LEADERSHIP
DARK MATTER

Leadership Dark Matter:
From Special Operations to Fortune 500

Paperback ISBN: 978-1-7348893-1-4
Hardcover ISBN: 978-1-7348893-0-7
E-book ISBN: 978-1-7348893-2-1

Visual credits: aurora (MikeDrago.cz/Shutterstock.com); mountains (moitumago/Shutterstock.com and Yoko Design/Shutterstock.com); people (Rawpixel.com/Shutterstock.com and Michal Sanca/Shutterstock.com); nature background (Jon Bilous/Shutterstock.com).

Design by: David Miles

LEADERSHIP
DARK MATTER

FROM SPECIAL OPERATIONS
TO FORTUNE 500

TONY MARINELLO

A gravitational force misunderstood
They require no recognition.
Universally important for the greater good
Others are always the mission.
They retain the milky way
And penetrate every thing.
Always willing to the lead the way
Influence is what they bring.
One is nature and one is nurture
But both are required by the people.
They are Occam's razor to the eternal searcher
And swear an oath to be fair and equal.
Both are humble and aware
Never afraid to fail, and always listen.
People are their umbel and they care
They never fade, they blaze the trail, they know
the mission.

CONTENTS

PROLOGUE

I am writing this book because being a leader is the most important role that any one person can hold, ever. History provides us with examples of leaders, such as generals, politicians, religious figures and activists, but we are rarely educated on how such leaders were developed. Biographies, third-party testimony and the media may provide glimpses of an individual leaders' motivation, upbringing or discipline. But there has yet to be an attempt to truly understand and educate potential leaders to maximize their human potential to become the leaders that the future demands. My intent in writing this book is to share my leadership perspective; create a guide that potential leaders, regardless of class, education or profession can understand; formalize leader creation education; and finally, provide best practices to leaders in any industry, position or staff capacity. This book does not apply to any specific trade, profession, gender or demographic. The topics and experiences herein simply cater to the leadership of the human dimension. The only customer of leadership is people, and only people can be leaders—everything else is an accessory.

Constantly evolving technology and stigmas regarding occupations or trades have resulted in leadership becoming an art that eludes most. Leadership is wildly misunderstood, and therefore leader development has become too compartmentalized. Bosses, positions, rank, and tenure have replaced true leadership. We would be smart to invest in leader development and readiness from the earliest possible age while maintaining a life-long learning attitude towards leadership. If the layperson from any nation, culture or demographic can see how overwhelmed and under-supported our leaders have become, then the person in a leadership position is not necessarily the problem. We need to take a step back, compose and remind ourselves of leadership fundamentals that we owe our developing and potential leaders.

Leaders are made, not born. The most critical time of development for potential leaders is their childhood and adolescence. Any personal leadership improvement past this point is built upon the foundation laid during this critical window. However, a person's upbringing is not their choice—it's the position they were placed in by their environment, their parents (or lack thereof) or generation. Therefore, leadership development and potential should be likened to learning a second language—people are more malleable and receptive to learning while in early development, but as we all know, we are still able to be molded and trained regardless of age.

I believe the development of true leadership requires struggle and example. Struggle and example have traditionally been provided to prospective leaders through their upbringing, conditioned by parenting and adjusted in adulthood. Some would argue that struggle and example cannot be replicated or taught, which is why it seems as though some people are just "natural born leaders" or that some leaders just contain those "intangible" leadership attributes. I would argue that both struggle and example can be replicated and provided into a learning environment. I will transform previously believed intangible leadership qualities into trainable and observable criteria to produce the strongest foundational leaders our country has observed.

Struggle is a constant attempt to stay afloat. For most, it's a financial hardship mitigated by physical labor. Financial hardship requires families to work tirelessly to provide and to sustain. That financial struggle is usually only maintained by relatively low-paying physical labor. Physical labor requires discipline, physical readiness, and resiliency. This blue-collar lifestyle requires an incredible amount of sacrifice. The sacrifices made by adults and parents are observed and conditioned by their children, which results in children developing a foundation of character. This should not be surprising. Leaders that come from this upbringing understand what working-class people need to prioritize first, how they communicate with each other, how to innovate and what is important in life.

Examples can be positive and negative, but both are valuable in leader development. Think about how you make judgments or how you make decisions. Most of the good judgment you exercise currently is based upon poor judgment you've exercised in the past. This is why losing is much more valuable than winning. What you gain from that poor example, bad decision or loss is the violence of that terrible feeling—it's a physical response. This is why we train, study or prepare so much better after a loss. We'll do anything not to feel that way again. Much like anything else, repetition is critical. The more you place yourself in an opportunity to lead or exercise judgment, and the more you fail or succeed, the more it will result in a lesson learned for your future development and improvement. However, as a child or even a young adult you are less likely to know the difference between a good and bad example for multiple reasons. First, you naturally assume that if an adult is doing it, it must be right or the best way to do whatever action you're observing. Next, you will likely have such a small group of adults or even peers to provide examples that bad examples are the only ones you observe, and you're none the wiser. Alternatively, you'll never realize the importance of experiencing a bad example, poor leader or loss until you observe a good example, true leader or win. It will be then that you truly gain an appreciation, perspective, and respect for leadership. Observing and witnessing a leader that provides a good example is life-changing.

INTRODUCTION

I genuinely and humbly feel that I have something to offer people regarding leadership. I come from an extremely hard-working, blue-collar family with members whom I have observed continuously improve their lives through struggle and adversity. Like most children, it wasn't until later in life that I appreciated my parents' resiliency, adaptability and work ethic. With that said, and when compared to some of the experiences or situations that other people face, my brother and I were blessed to have two loving parents that provided anything and everything they could for our betterment. There are plenty of other families and people that have or currently do struggle at a level that I cannot truly relate to. But I do understand sacrifice—moving from home to apartment and back based on financial struggle, and experiencing the cable or electricity being canceled because the bill couldn't be paid. My parents were constantly working in order to provide, and I was completely oblivious to it because my parents still attempted to provide everything possible to my brother and me to be successful and happy. Their ability to overcome adversity through laughter and maintaining a sense of humor has had the biggest impact on me. You can't bring them down.

I first realized that we "had less" or may have been punching above our weight class at about nine or ten years old. At the age of eight, I developed a passion for ice hockey because of the movie Mighty Ducks. I told my parents I wanted to play hockey, to which they immediately said yes, having no idea how to begin, register, where in the area it was played or most importantly how they would find the money and time to support it. As I reflect, this is when my leadership experience and journey began. I played travel hockey for sixteen years—a time in which I watched my parents spend thousands of dollars they didn't have for equipment, travel and vehicles. They even moved to another town to provide my brother and me an opportunity to attend a school with hockey (among other reasons). I grew up playing hockey, and most of my friends derived from it—some of whom are still playing professionally. I played through high school, played junior hockey for two years in what was called the Eastern Junior Hockey League (EJHL) and then four years of DIV III NCAA Collegiate Hockey.

In order to pay for college, I was forced to take out multiple loans, which I just finished paying. It took me eleven years to pay off in-state tuition—the education system in America requires a completely separate book to explain. Every summer I would work construction—specifically, framing houses and roofs to maintain. This was also one of the most rewarding times of my life and acted as another pillar in my development as a successful leader. Learning a trade is completely invaluable. I would argue one of the most humbling aspects of life is working with your hands, and we'll speak more about the importance of labor trades in this book. The discipline, work ethic, mental and physical toughness that my parents instilled in me made hockey a natural fit and extremely fulfilling. Those attributes were fine-tuned, improved and challenged while learning a trade.

In my last year of undergraduate studies, I came to terms with the idea that almost twenty years of competitive sport, preparation and readiness was coming to an end, and I needed to find another source of competition, self-improvement, and challenge. This is a difficult time for collegiate athletes who do not have the intestinal fortitude or self-awareness to be honest with themselves. Some will chase a dream of playing at a level everyone knows that can't achieve or limit their overall talent to be successful in a single, recreational sports industry. If they were honest with themselves, they could transition the energy and effort exerted in that sport to something different, as the possibility of success for them is high. However, people are scared of the unknown and sometimes even expend their curiosity or goal-achieving attitude too soon, resulting in their mediocrity and complacency later in life. Personally, I knew early that I didn't have the natural ability to play at the highest possible professional level and therefore strived for a challenge in every possible dimension—physical, mental, emotional—outside of a game or a sport. After one of my last hockey games as a senior, I told my parents I was going to join the Army. My mother immediately threatened to disown me.

I decided to pursue a graduate degree to further my education experience, join the Army's Reserve Officer Training Corps (ROTC) and began boxing. Despite the advice given to me to pursue a specific, "career-enhancing degree," such as an MBA or MPA, I deliberately chose a Liberal Arts degree. Regarding the education of leaders, I truly believe it's much more valuable to be versed in a plethora of topics and subjects versus being specifically trained in one area that you may or may not pursue or enjoy. Additionally, studying humanities creates a shared understanding of people. I believe this prepares potential leaders well to relate and empathize with people. Great leaders can lead anyone in any industry, regardless of degree type. Why not understand a little about a lot versus a lot about a little? This will have to be a deliberate choice for you. Is it more important to you to have a degree(s) that people recommend based on a specific career choice with the intent of achieving a certain salary? Or is it more important to you that you have a degree that may provide you the ability to better the human experience in any career choice with the intent of achieving a greater purpose?

Most people who have the privilege to pursue an advanced education show passion for their work and perform well. The real difference between undergraduate and graduate work is in graduate work you are truly interested in the topics you are reading, writing and discussing. This should be expected, as it's the topic you chose to pursue versus a smattering of general education topics experienced with undergraduate degrees. While pursuing topics such as emergency preparedness, sociology, and public administration, I focused most of my effort and interest in intelligence studies. My goal was to commission as an Intelligence Officer in the Army. While pursuing that goal, I needed a physical and mental challenge that was different from the

Army and a graduate degree. I began boxing before my first year of graduate school and learned first fist (get it? Instead of first hand? No? Okay, moving on...) that combat sports differ significantly from team sports. I believe that team sports provide a more complete and fundamental foundation for leadership. Team sports are amazing to participate in at a young age because they establish both your identity and teamwork. They allow us to focus on a team goal, and most importantly, the role the team needs you to assume for the greater good while pursuing victory.

Individual sports are ideal for individual accountability and self-improvement. Your efforts receive direct and immediate feedback, there is no one else to blame but yourself. Training for individual sports, specifically individual combat sports, is tailorable to you and allows you to gain a level of self-awareness that is very difficult to achieve otherwise. This is because of one word—pain. Any shortcuts you decide to take, you will pay for in pain. If you believe you have trained yourself to a level of competence in a certain area, you'll find out immediately when someone stands across from you. Individual competence and readiness feedback is slightly more difficult in a team environment because of the conditions of the sport, how the game is played, and how both teams have to provide the opportunity to an individual, such as a penalty shot in hockey, a free throw in basketball, an individual brief or project in business, etc. The absolute most valuable aspect of an individual combat sport is the mental composure and decision making under fire it enables.

Organizations hire and pay large sums of money to understand and train people to make decisions, regardless of industry. Do you want to know the best way to prepare yourself for making a decision under pressure? Get punched in the face by someone who wants to do you harm for that decision. The composure you acquire from this type of training is invaluable. You will graduate from making a decision to making the right decision, or you'll learn that you are not ready to be in a position to make said decision—all of which are critical to know about yourself in reference to leadership. It will also prepare you with a level of mental resilience that simply can't be trained in any other way. Are you able to maintain your composure—physically, mentally and emotionally while literally under attack? The mental agility, adaptability, and resiliency I developed in years of hockey and learning a trade directly correlated with my ability to quickly improve in boxing and learn leadership with the Army. The additional discipline and candid feedback I received also directly affected my graduate work. I was performing at a high level. As a result of those efforts, in 2010 I went undefeated in the Amateur Golden Glove Adirondack Region of NY state and commissioned as a Distinguished Military Graduate in the Army as an Active Duty Military Intelligence Officer.

THERE'S THE ARMY AND THERE'S THE 75TH RANGER REGIMENT

My newly married wife and I had just moved from New York to Arizona. I was nervous about what life in the Army was going to be like. I had no frame of reference for whether or not I fit the mold of an Army Officer, a Leader or an Intelligence Professional, but I was eager to learn and prove myself. At this point in my life, I was a bit older than other junior officers given the year I took off between high school and college to play junior hockey and my two additional years of graduate school. After about four or so months into my initial Officer training, I realized that although likeminded and motivated people surrounded me, I still desired a physical and intellectual challenge I had yet to experience. Around this time, I was informed that the 75th Ranger Regiment was coming to the installation to recruit Officers, and I jumped at the opportunity.

I knew immediately that I wanted to assess for the 75th Ranger Regiment when I saw the Officer and Noncommissioned Officer they sent as a recruitment team. Their individual discipline, physical appearance, humble confidence, and quiet professionalism drew me to the unit. Little did I know, I was going to develop an outstanding personal and professional relationship with that Noncommissioned Officer that would last to this day. After a rigorous assessment and selection process, I was chosen for continued service and selection to the 75th Ranger Regiment. The "chosen for continued service and selection" statement means I made it through the very first gate. I was good enough to be considered for the actual tryout. My next step was to attend the world's most famous and infamous leadership school—Ranger School.

What is Ranger School? It's a school that will push you to an absolute physical and mental limit. Ranger School will reveal your true identity. You will learn more about yourself, the human spirit, and the importance of teamwork and mission completion in that time than any other time in your life. It's beyond my writing ability to describe the levels of sleep and food deprivation and the miraculous ability your body has to grow things on it you didn't even know existed (and then recover). And to mitigate any doubt, "droning" is real. It is absolutely possible for you to walk and talk with 100 lbs. on your back and be completely asleep. I have seen Rangers walk off small cliffs, walk-in neck-deep in swamps, march completely naked in the middle of tropical storms with just a camelback, give tactical instructions to Rangers in their rack—all while 100% asleep. I have observed a Ranger Instructor (RI)—whom our squad called "Earnest goes to Ranger School" because he looked like the main character from the Earnest movies—be evacuated because he had a core temperature over 105 degrees, which is life-threatening. The backstory was he had "walked" us, meaning we just ruck marched with our equipment through the jungle for just shy of 24 hrs. When he put us down to sleep at about 0230 with the intent to wake us up at 0430, I woke up to the most blood curdling, male scream I have ever heard in my life at 0330. This was the sound Earnest made when a thermometer was shoved in his ass to check his core temperature. Not knowing what happened, my squad thought one of two things occurred 1) Ranger was droning (sleepwalking) and walked into a branch and lost his eye or 2) Ranger found out that another Ranger was the reason he didn't pass his patrol or was "No-Go'd"—which would require him to be recycled to the beginning of Ranger School or kicked out—and therefore killed this other Ranger.

I also observed my "Ranger Buddy" get either stung or bitten in the dick by a scorpion. It was hilarious. We woke up in the Florida jungle, he turned to me and said: "Ranger Buddy, something bit me in the dick." Keep in mind, by this time in Ranger School, your body is emaciated and you can identify other Rangers without seeing them based on their smell (this happens when your body resorts to burning muscle due to a lack of caloric intake and lack of sleep). When that happens, your body releases a terrible ammonia smell. If you combine that with already existing body odor, walking through the worst possible terrain and swamps, then you can understand why we would burn our uniforms after. Before you leave on patrol, there is usually a medic to help Rangers diagnose whatever may be growing on them during that week, help Ranger's peel off two-inch flaps of skin from their feet if they got trench foot, give prednisone shots to those that have been sleeping in poison oak or sumac and monitor bites.

My Ranger Buddy approached this medic while the medic sat in a field chair and we walked through to see him like we were at a soup kitchen. While the medic was turned around, retrieving something from his aid and litter bag, my Ranger Buddy stepped in front of him and when the medic turned back around to see the next Ranger, he was met eye level with a penis that had a scorpion bite on it. This, hands down, was one of my best days in Ranger School—it was epically hilarious. The medic gave a short, manly yelp and fell back out of his field chair. The medic composed himself reacquired his military bearing and advised that my Ranger Buddy be taken out of the course to monitor his...bite. To which my Ranger Buddy said "absolutely not!" He had been waiting for his roster number to be called to lead a patrol in a leadership position before graduating, and he was not willing to let a bite take a Ranger tab away from him.

After a brief, sideline discussion with the Ranger Instructor, they allowed him to stay, but the medic required that a black circle be drawn around the bite with a permanent marker. This would allow

LEADERSHIP DARK MATTER

other medics and Ranger Buddies to observe how the bite swelled, which would indicate how serious the wound was or if it was getting infected, etc. My Ranger Buddy returned to our ten-person squad in complete relief for not being dropped from the course. After asking me to be his Team Leader, he asked me how the hell he was going to monitor this bite while being tasked with a leadership position during the day. I hesitated for 10 seconds and said: "Ranger Buddy—today, we're going dicks out." We told each Ranger in our squad that for the day, all ten of us will be conducting the day's events with our dicks out of our pants. It was met with immediate buy-in and committed compliance, not a single question. If our Ranger buddy needs our support, and uniformity is important—then there would be zero questions, consider it done. On a serious note, it was pretty medically sound. Think about how much heat you compile in your crotch and therefore how easy it was to regulate your temperature by keeping your fly open. At this point in the School, we were losing a handful of Rangers every day due to heat casualties. It was June in the Florida jungle, and our class had gone from about 500 to 100. So, there we were, for a 24-hr. period, running around in the jungle with our dicks out in support of our Ranger Buddy, periodically checking his bite to see if and how it was swelling. Every time a Ranger Instructor would say "Ranger, is your fucking dick out?" our immediate response would be "Roger, Sergeant—we're regulating our temperatures and supporting a Ranger Buddy"—to which they would either say "get the fuck away from me" or "drive-on" or "put your dick back in your pants, Ranger." We would comply with the latter if directed, but would just take them out once they walked away.

In retrospect, I had a blast at Ranger School. Sure, I lost enamel on my teeth, probably stunted my growth due to the compression of my spine by carrying all that weight, lost around thirty pounds the worst way possible, but also made lifetime friends with people whom I would never have interacted with otherwise. I remember carrying a Ranger to the medical station from our sleeping area. It seemed like a mile because he snapped his ankle while running in the attempt to get a good sleeping spot. About a year later, he wrote me a hand-written letter thanking me for what I had done. He had remembered how many Rangers ran directly past him and left him there to figure it out for himself because the school had just started and everyone was worried about themselves first. Most of Ranger School is just about staying healthy enough to make it through. I have countless stories like these from Ranger School. The bottom line is what brings people close together—regardless of industry or job description—is observing the best and the worst of each other. Exposing yourself, including your weaknesses and vulnerabilities, removes any barriers you have consciously or subconsciously created, and your team begins to flourish and perform at a remarkably high level.

I'll make one last attempt to create an understanding of what Ranger School is like. You know when you're watching some type of action film and a song is loudly played that is designed to motivate you during a time of extreme difficulty and adversity? It allows you to almost visualize yourself in that scenario and convince yourself of how you would perform and respond. Yeah, so reality is nothing like that. I so badly wanted my mind and psyche to play the countless songs I had heard in movies to motivate me through a terrible situation but it never happened. In fact, it's the complete opposite—its dead silent. For me, it was humbling and I'll never forget it. Nature doesn't care if you live or die. Its purpose will be completed regardless of your anguish, presence or actions. If your will and grit to press on doesn't ignite you to move, maintain momentum and persevere, then you'll just be part of 99% of Americans who have thought about completing something amazing like Ranger School, but never will. With all that being said, it was just a school, and if you have a good group of guys (and now girls) to go through with you, it's easy, and you'd be surprised what your mind, body, and spirit will adjust to. School is not real life—don't be the person who measures himself or herself on his or her school performance because school, especially Ranger School, is just another minimum threshold you need to pass to make it to the real thing.

My successful completion of Ranger School meant that I was one step closer to being a member of the 75th Ranger Regiment. And just to clarify, there has always been a misunderstanding about the difference between a Ranger School Graduate and being a Ranger in the 75th Ranger Regiment. It's a point of confusion for some people, even in the Army, so I will try to make it as clear as possible. The general-purpose Army is the owner and maintainer of Ranger School. Service members of any military branch or specialty can attend Ranger School if they are supported and endorsed by their respective chains of command. Graduates of Ranger School receive the Ranger Tab, which they wear on their uniforms. This should not be in any way confused with being a Ranger from the 75th Ranger Regiment. For most, being a Ranger School graduate is impressive enough and is indeed an honor. However, the Ranger tab is the absolute bare minimum requirement to be a member of the 75th Ranger Regiment. Being a Ranger in the 75th Ranger Regiment means you are a four-time volunteer. Members volunteer to join the Army, volunteer to attend Airborne School (jump out of planes), volunteer to go to Ranger School and volunteer to be a member in one of America's most elite, professional and competent special operations fighting forces the world has ever seen. For some people, a task (or accomplishment, depending on how you look at it) like Ranger School is a culminating life event. For others, it was just a time in your life when you enjoyed being tested. Truthfully, I barely think about it anymore. It's not as hard as people make it out to be. It was just a requirement to meet a desired end state. The experience of School was valuable; the tab that's worn after completion is a piece of cloth. Real Rangers would tell you that the tab itself doesn't matter; the experience does.

Part of my selection process to become a member of the 75th Ranger Regiment was that I would serve for a year in Korea in order to understand the basic functionality of the Army, military intelligence and leadership. I will always be thankful for my time in Korea. The leadership I was exposed to and the coaching I received from Noncommissioned Officers and Warrant Officers was truly rewarding. The personal experiences I gained helped shape me into the man I am today. My wife and I were able to travel throughout South Korea, Thailand and China. I have resounding memories of Korea that bring a smile every time I think about them, such as our first Korean driving experience and the day I disrespected a bathroom designated for a Korean General.

I arrived in Korea before my wife, in-processed the unit and installation and found a place to live. My wife and I were excited to live in Korea—not on the installation, but in town. We lived in a small apartment less than a mile away from the post. Now that we were off post, we needed a car. I bought what Soldiers call a Korea Car immediately for about $1000. The white Hyundai needed some basic level maintenance, so on the day I picked up my wife from Seoul International Airport, we immediately drove to a Korean body shop and got it serviced. I distinctly remember two things about this day. First, driving in Korea is an emotional experience, there is almost no respect or enforcement for traffic laws. You are taking your life in your hands every time you get into a car. Second, it was ridiculously hot and humid on the June day. After sitting in the waiting room with my wife who just arrived in the country, I decided I needed water immediately. I took a glass bottle that said *fresh* on it out of a refrigerator in the body shop and proceeded to slam it down my gullet. Have you ever drunk something so aggressively that you don't even give your sense of taste the ability to weight in? That's exactly what I did. After two to three American sized chugs, I realize…this is liquor. It was Soju, a clear, colorless Korean rice liquor with an alcohol content that varies from around 16-50%. Thirty minutes later, I knew I couldn't drive out of the body shop. So, I told my wife to get behind the wheel within her first three hours in Korea without a license. I gave her a quick rundown of the differences/risks of driving in Korea versus home. She immediately started the car and backed into a brick wall behind the body shop and leaped to traffic resembling a Mario cart video game.

As a young Intelligence Platoon Leader, I learned equipment accountability, logistics, basic leadership skills, analytical tradecraft and the purpose of a staff. My role in Korea was to augment and support Korean intelligence and war-fighters with timely and accurate intelligence. We did this by deploying a team of Soldiers with field-expedite and tactical intelligence systems designed to function in any environment. I was responsible for manning, training and equipping my platoon to execute a plan and we would rehearse, improve and repeat. Our most common mission would be to co-locate with a Korean element or installation to cross-train and provide capabilities briefs to Korean (ROK) military officials. We would conduct our missions on their installations, meaning we would eat with them and sleep in their barracks (if we didn't sleep outside). I will never forget a mission that required us to participate in the 2012 Seoul Nuclear Summit. My platoon was tasked with providing support to a Korean installation and we set up our equipment in the middle of what looked to be a parade field.

The next morning, I was woken up to a brigade-size element of around 3,000 South Korean Soldiers conducting a unit run. I looked out the window to see the entirety of the brigade running with their shirts off in the middle of March. I quickly shrugged it off and got dressed for breakfast. As we entered their dining facility, we realized that every meal would consist of primarily water, fish soup, rice and kimchi. On the second day, walking back from lunch, my stomach revealed how pissed off it was that I had put it through this drastic change, and it felt as though a cinder block had dropped from the top of my stomach. I ran to the bathroom. When I entered a bathroom in the Korean Headquarters building, I was immediately surprised by the number of people utilizing it. I now understand that Koreans are very good about dental hygiene and it is customary that a large group of people utilize the bathroom to brush their teeth, etc. right after a meal. I immediately looked for a stall, all of which were taken—and knew this was going to be bad.

I noticed one of the bathroom stall doors was made of wood and was considerably nicer than the others, I immediately entered and shut the door, tore my uniform off like they were tear-away pants and sat down. Once I sat down, I realized that this toilet was like nothing I had ever seen. There were buttons and switches all around the seat. I reminded myself that Korean technology such as phones and appliances were usually better than ours, so I got over it pretty quickly. I saw a button that I thought was a heater and pressed it with the intent of improving a situation that was already pretty embarrassing and explosive. When I touched that button, it sounded as though a sprinkler system of a professional football stadium was being initiated. I immediately had the urge to stand up and once I did, with almost zero clothes on, a stream of hot water from what seemed to be a firehouse projected from the toilet, hitting the top of the wood door in front of me spraying in every direction.

After what seemed like an eternity and in slow motion, I reached for the toilet seat and slammed it shut to prevent any more water from coming out of this Korean toilet aka super soaker. Keep in mind, I still hadn't gone to the bathroom at this point, so I was a little wet from the firehose, 90% naked and completely sweating. I opened the bathroom door to every Korean that was in the bathroom looking directly at me, motionless with toothbrushes sticking out their mouths and the sinks running. I buried my head, shimmied to the next, non-fancy and more traditional stall and downloaded at a ferocious pace. With what I believed to be the worst behind me, I start my scan for toilet paper...nothing, why *would* there be toilet paper. In a full panic, and while water is still likely dripping down the door of my previous stall, I start wargaming a potential solution. I could just put my hand under the walls of the stall to my sides and ask for toilet paper—nope, the side walls are down the ground. I could just yell for TP in the hope that any human soul would help me from outside—nope, I'm in a foreign country and the likelihood of them speaking English is low. Final answer: I got it, I should take my knife off my pants, and cut my undershirt into a belly shirt and use that as toilet paper; What is yes for $600 please, Alex.

And that's exactly what I did. I can't imagine what Korean Soldiers in the other stalls could have been thinking at this point. All they were hearing was this meat-head American, clearly cutting some type of fabric in their Headquarters bathroom. I did what I needed to do, stood up, composed myself and flushed. As with most flushes, you don't usually stick around to confirm completion. So, once I hit the flush handle, I opened the door and the boys were still out there, eyes wide open, staring at me. I heard a terrible gurgling sound behind me and I look back to see the toilet clogged—the shitty-shirt combo was too much for it. I made a decision right then that I wouldn't regret—I ran. As I was running out of this bathroom, I noticed the original stall I had assaulted, the one with the wooden door, had 4-stars on it. Meaning, it was the Korean Generals stall. I'll never forget it. Sorry, Korea.

My time was coming to an end in Korea, and the Regiment notified me that I was slotted for an upcoming Ranger Assessment and

Selection date. This was the final test to gain entry into the Regiment. I am unwilling to divulge specific details regarding the assessment and selection process in order to maintain the integrity of the selection, but I will say it is intellectually and professionally difficult. Also, if you are not physically prepared—you'll be seriously injured. The professionalism and competence of the Regiment's Noncommissioned Officer Corps are some of the many reasons why it's one of the most lethal organizations in the world. And that was immediately on display during this course. Regardless of how you perform in the course, all candidates are required to conduct a final board or interview. This board consists of the Regiment's most senior and experienced professionals and is the most intense, humbling and sobering experience most will have in their professional careers. I distinctly remember sitting in what seemed to be the center of a small room, surrounded by men that had fought our nation's most difficult, unspoken or unacknowledged battles as they passed judgment on my performance and potential. I knew I barely deserved to be the same room as them, but I figured being a college athlete and a Golden Glove boxer with a master's degree should at least make me a contender. Their ability to candidly yet professionally dismantle my academic and physical performance as well as my leadership potential will remain the most humbling experience I will ever encounter in my life. Even though I was selected for hire as an intelligence officer, I walked out of that room feeling confident that I should kill myself. It was the worst I had ever felt after winning.

I am unable to display in words my level of gratitude and appreciation to the 75th Ranger Regiment. The consistent level of leadership, intelligence, readiness, and potential is truly difficult to describe. Every single Ranger I encountered had a story, much like all people, but hearing and observing the motivation of Ranger is like something out of a blockbuster film. With close to ten years in the Army, my most honored and cherished memories are from the Regiment, more specifically the Rangers themselves. 99.9% of Americans and even service members have no idea the type of people I am referring to here. Civilians attempt to understand or attempt to relate with past athletic experiences or by imagining to the best of their ability what I am describing but have no real way to conceptualize the professionalism, furiousness, competence, grit, and unity of these men (and now women). These quiet professionals purposely refrain from the limelight in order to maintain operational security and represent the integrity of the special operations community.

With that said, I believe the organization should make a more deliberate effort to tell the public about its history and current role in the world. If the Regiment were to apply its prowess to doing this correctly, I believe it would result in a significant increase in recruitment and retention. It is my opinion that the Regiment has purposely and professionally veered away from public recognition or telling its war stories because it's simply not in its nature to seek recognition. The Regiment has work to do—the most difficult work there is to be done. Doing bad things to bad people and answering the call of the nation, where ever it may be. I have sat back and observed other organizations produce multiple books and blockbuster films as the Regiment stands aside reminding itself how those occurrences *actually* unfolded or about the countless examples of gallantry, bravery, and sacrifice that have never been repeated. The Regiment would do well by its current and incoming Rangers by making its history a priority. There are incredible roles that the Regiment as played in history that its members are unaware of. Much like any other wildly successful organization or Fortune 500 company, it is frequently consumed by the tyranny of the present. But I understand why this is the case. It's difficult to stop and look behind you while sprinting forward under load, towards the danger on uneven terrain, and in terrible conditions while every other living being is running away from it.

The first person I saw as I walked into the Ranger Regiment with a tan beret was a close friend whom I met throughout the assessment and selection process and in Ranger School. The Army provides these unexpected and emotional reunions often, because it spans the globe, but is also an extremely small community. He was now a senior Noncommissioned Officer and I walked up on him just outside the battalion headquarters building as he was screaming at two Military Police (MP) Officers for hastily parking beyond the Battalion Commanders vehicle. I wasn't surprised at all and laughed as I said "Ranger Buddy" loudly while approaching him from beyond while his finger was in the face of the MP's. Honestly, the reason I essentially yelled before reaching him was to ensure he wasn't surprised. I didn't want him to throw a haymaker at me and then have to explain why I was knocked out by an NCO on my first day. While one of the MPs attempted to inject a respectful word, my Ranger Buddy turned and saw me, embraced me with a huge hug and said "Ranger Buddy! Welcome to the varsity, Sir."

Simultaneously, two new Ranger privates pulled into the single visitor parking spot next to the battalion commanders' vehicle, just missing the MP's vehicle. As they approached, My Ranger Buddy ensured they presented the proper salute and shared the greeting of the day to me. He asked them if they had "seriously just parking in front of the battalion headquarters." The privates were new, had no idea what they had done wrong and snapped to parade rest (a modified position of attention). In so many words, my Ranger Buddy had informed them that the parking spot in question was for actual visitors, which they were not. He then told the new Rangers to conduct lunges back to their vehicle, find the farthest parking spot available and lunge all the way back to him—they had 2 minutes. The young Rangers, likely high school star athletes or even young professionals before being honored with a tan beret, replied with "Roger Sergeant" and starting lunging away. He then put his arm around my shoulder and said: "Follow me, Sir." The two MPs were still standing there, not having said a word and turned toward my Ranger Buddy as we walked past them, eager to state their business but not daring to say a word in fear of taking a Ranger NCO off task.

I distinctly remember every Ranger Officer and Noncommissioned Officer looking me up and down as I walked in the battalion area as if I was unworthy or edible. There was a bravado of excellence in the air that I simply can't describe. I knew then that every single day, event or even task would be closely watched, evaluated and judged. I knew how I completed those tasks would slowly develop into my reputation—and in a community as small this, your reputation is everything. First impressions are lasting and perception is reality until proven otherwise. I was constantly assessed—from the way I looked in and out of uniform, the way I ate, you name it. I was naïve enough to think that I would earn significant credibility once we started to conduct physical training together. I had always outperformed my peers physically and was confident my physical performance would at least create some white space for me to contribute something significant.

My confidence was misplaced. The next day, we ran eight miles and I was struggling to maintain the pace of the other Rangers, which seemed to be no slower than a seven-minute mile. I have always prided myself on my attention to detail and observation. I can retain an incredible amount of detail when it came to interacting with people. And during this run/introduction, I observed their gaits and posture with awe. I clearly understood this to be an unspoken initiation and was immediately humbled by the realization that I wasn't nearly as good as I thought I was. I was intellectually humbled daily as well. I have noticed both in and out of the Army that people usually associate intelligence or life experience with rank, position or title, and it is an absolute recipe for failure. I distinctly remember giving an intelligence assessment to an Infantry Sergeant (E5, a relatively junior Noncommissioned Officer) thinking it was more than sufficient and that he might have even been impressed. Wrong again. After patiently and professionally listening and waiting for me to finish, he replied with a respectful, well-spoken rebuttal that was more accurate than my assessment. I was floored, genuinely impressed and thankful for his perspective. In a later conversation, he went on to tell me that after playing on the Division I squash team at Princeton University, he worked on Wall Street before decided to join the Ranger Regiment directly after 9/11.

The Regiment is filled with individuals like the one I just described, star athletes (Pat Tillman, Alejandro Villanueva) and endurance athletes, some of whom rendered immediate aid during the Boston Marathon bombing. Top-tier academic talents in both the enlisted and Commissioned ranks from the best universities and businesses in the country. One of the Rangers in the company I commanded spoke seven languages, and after immigrating to this country from a historic, war-torn part of India, he earned a business a degree and worked for Verizon for years before deciding he needed more of a challenge. A close friend of mine and fellow intelligence officer decided to leave the Army and received a full academic scholarship to Stanford Law School. I have served with incredible staff officers who have shown unbelievable gallantry in battle, earning the Silver Star and then going on to become Downing Scholars, attending the Kennedy School and Tufts for their graduate work before returning to the Regiment.

It's difficult to limit my writing here because I would genuinely like to tell about every single Regimental interaction that I can remember as they have all made such lasting impressions on me. I truly believe that the men I have had the honor of serving with are superhuman. Countless times, I have reflected upon how lucky I was to be serving with such talented leaders, operators and staff members. Serving in the 75th Ranger Regiment was the most rewarding experience of my life. It was filled with such passion and excellence. People of this caliber are truly rare, and it's amazing to see how they rise to the occasion and improve when around each other. They cannot help to compete and win in all forms of life. However, I will say that men and women of this caliber are incapable of being mediocre and sometimes that results in incredible tragedy. The reality is that each and every Ranger lives on either side of the societal spectrum. None of them live in the middle. They live on a balance beam of wild, unlimited success or rock-bottom failure or loss. Ranger lives his life full throttle at all times; it's what separates them from regular humans. Whenever they choose, they will decide to attend Harvard Business School or the Kennedy School of Government, or deliberately decide to success-fully execute an audacious bank robbery. They will become direct liaisons to the President or they will get so intoxicated that they fall out of a vehicle while driving 80 miles per hour and are killed by an eighteen-wheeler. These men live in absolute extremes.

I have thought pretty long about why this is the case, and the only answer I can come up with is that we were born in the wrong generation. I look at the careers of professional Officers and Noncommissioned Officers who have served for twenty-plus years and have deployed no less than fifteen times and think that they are reincarnated leaders and warriors from our planets most difficult and brutal battles. I look at my generation and see a level of servanthood and grit that resembles Americans in World War II. These men and women simply can't assimilate into a 9-to-5 job or social media ex-istence. It's no different than attempting to tame a completely wild and dangerous animal. Any limitation or confinement completely dampens their spirit, intellectual capacity, and emotional freedom.

I have seen great men, fathers, and husbands die in training and combat, terrorists being served justice, and innocent children and women killed. I have seen Rangers die, when not deployed, out of pure boredom. I have seen men look for ways to lead others while trying to lead themselves around PTSD.

Men born in the wrong generation, who struggle to meander through life when not in combat or completing a meaningful task. I've walked in places that look like the lunar surface, having no idea how one planet and its people can be so completely different from each other. I've participated in events in awe of Ranger, like running eleven miles in remembrance of 9/11 with a gas mask on, while carrying a full-size American Flag on a highway without breaking a stride. I have told parents their children were injured; I have advocated for missions that have resulted in the death of young Americans. My wife and I have fostered and housed sexually abused and neglected children. I was in an aircraft that almost crashed in contested air space. I have seen limbs and bones broken and smashed due to jumping out of airplanes. In fact, I remember a time my wife calling me from the hospital where she was a registered nurse, and asking what the hell we were doing. Because a guy wearing the same type of non-standard uniform she had seen me in before, came into the hospital on a stretcher with his feet on backward. This was due to losing air under his parachute that resulted in him plummeting to the ground and landing heels first on an airfield tarmac. I've watched competent people be fired and removed for lapses in judgment. I have received an overwhelming amount of trust by leaders allowing me to join them in places and meetings that I probably shouldn't have been involved in. I've laughed and bled with superhumans on target. Don't let me confuse you—I have never been seriously injured. I have friends that have been shot and or lost limbs when I fell on my face while walking to a target. And when I got up, after letting the powdered dust and sand settle, I watched my friends and fellow Rangers bent over in laughter as I stuck my finger through the flesh between my nose and upper lip.

My last official duty in the Army and the 75th Ranger Regiment was as a pallbearer for a friend, a fellow Ranger Officer and his two beautiful daughters who were killed in a tragic car accident during Memorial Day weekend. He, his daughters and eldest son were driving across the country to their next duty station after he had just graduated from Duke with his master's degree. This terrible tragedy occurred while his wife and newborn son unknowingly flew across the country to meet the rest of the family. I watched and failed to hold back my emotion as leaders from the Regiment gave his young son, the sole survivor from the accident, a folded flag in remembrance of his father's service. I watched our nation's strongest, bravest and most resilient warrior, a Ranger Wife, graciously accept a folded flag and console her remaining son and newborn child with pride and bravery. I have seen and participated in incredible violence and loss but have also seen the very best our nation has to offer. Words will never describe my appreciation for the leadership, strength, and sacrifice of our spouses.

INTRO TO LEADERSHIP

With a lifetime of leadership experiences in competitive athletics, military special operations and now in the business world, I would like to offer leadership lessons that I have observed and practiced. My genuine intent here is to provide leadership from my perspective hoping that it will resonate with people and professionals in all positions and industries. I, in no way, believe or assess that I have leadership figured out and that the following is an all-encompassing recipe for unbridled leadership success. There is plenty that I still have to learn about leadership, myself and ways to influence others. But I do believe my life experiences are extremely rare, valuable and critical to leaders of all kinds.

What does a leader do? What is a leader for? Leaders create influence and purpose in people. Leadership is both an art and a science. If art is the application of human expression in creation and science is knowledge acquired through observation and experiment, then potential leaders should seek to refine and improve both aspects while leading. A leader that only acknowledges the art of leadership is likely good at motivating others to work together towards a common goal, but will fail to understand the specifics of their industry or their employee's experiences and struggles. Leaders that only focus on the science of leadership likely see their employees as a number, a metric employed to increase other metrics - such as profit. We have all experienced a leader make an "Art" based decision, such as changing a business practice or process with little to no insight as to the technical repercussions or cost such as monetary cost, time requirement, and human labor. Their intent was likely genuine, but their lack of understanding probably resulted in critical corner-cutting, long-term loss, or just plain confusion. For example, think about a boss that took the time to question their lowest level employee regarding a business practice and that employee recommended a change. The boss, with noble and genuine intent, agreed with the employee and immediately institutes a change in process and requires each one of his middle-level leaders to comply. Because that boss didn't take the time to understand the science of that decision through observation and experiment, middle-level management or ground-level leaders feel as though their boss doesn't trust them. The ground level leaders may feel that their boss doesn't understand the second and third-order effects of that decision, which results in the boss losing credibility.

We have also seen "Science"-based decisions that leave us wondering how in the world this person was placed in a position to make such decisions. These types of decisions are made more commonly then the business world would like to admit. An example of a "Science" decision would be something like... "X metrics indicate that if an additional, more complex digital tracker is used to compile an already digitally tracked metric, then our low performance in this area should improve." Upon receipt of this information, "Science" leaders (or bosses as I call them) quickly err on the side of the metrics, immediately approve what they believe will correct the issue and then vehemently enforce its adoption and use. This boss takes almost no time—or worse, doesn't care what the user level experience will be, let alone researching a separate reason for the assessed low compliance or performance. If it is even suspected that the use of this additional tool will increase productivity, then it's endorsed.

These types of analytical and quantifiable metrics are likely compiled over time by staff members whose sole focus are numbers. These staff members, who again genuinely believe they are improving the company by recommending this seemingly simple addition, likely have zero frame of reference as to the five W's—who, what, when, where and most importantly, why. Why is the metric in question low? Who is currently responsible for the original performance and who will become responsible once this "Science"-based recommendation is made? What about it makes it important? When did low performance begin, when will this "fix" be employed and what are the tertiary effects of the decision? All of these questions will have to be answered by the company's lowest level leaders, who are the ones completing the mission or task of the company or element. The "Science" boss places this great idea on the shoulders of their subordinate leaders, already overwhelmed by the amount of metrics, reports, and requirements they have to complete.

True leaders understand the value of art and science in leadership and use both to influence people. Employing both the art and science of leadership is extremely difficult. Most people are unable to consciously balance these two aspects of leadership because every single leadership interaction, engagement or situation requires various amounts of either art or science to resolve. Leaders must realize that their ground-level leaders are constantly sprinting with a plate of grapes. If unsupported and unguided, they will prioritize the grapes that can stay on the plate and identify which grapes can fall...and grapes have to fall. It's impossible for them not to. It's a leader's role to give clear, concise priorities, expectations and make their subordinate leaders understand where they and the organization can assume risk. It's also a leader's role to protect their ground-level and mid-level leaders. If you're in a leadership position right now and you don't know what I'm talking about here, you're a boss. And if you're a boss, you probably think things are going better than they are...they aren't. Your leaders have just decided that you can't fix, resolve and help them with their problems, so they stopped coming to you. There is no better indicator of whether you are an effective leader or not. If your people stop coming to you with issues or problems, it's not because they don't exist, it's because they don't trust that you'll do anything about them.

There is a direct correlation between how effective you are as a leader and how many problems you field. If your leaders are coming to you with problems it's because they think you can provide a solution. That means either you or your position has established trust. Leaders can turn that trust into loyalty by mentoring those junior leaders to not only bring you problems but also to lead through that problem when you aren't there. That's development. For example, if within the first month of you serving in a leadership position, no one comes to you for help, that's fine. It's because they are observing your observance and assessing your assessment. If in the second month, they come to you for your perspective or feedback, then you did something in your first month to draw them in. If you have shown a level of servanthood and genuine concern, it will be clear to those leaders. If in the third month, you field their concerns and problems, and instead of giving them the solution, you teach them how to identify the root cause, weigh available options and finally make an educated recommendation for your decision, they will have learned that you care about their development and betterment. Before you know it (and sometimes before you are ready for it), these junior leaders will find solutions to problems you didn't know existed and they will come to you to ensure you were aware of their decision.

You have just developed a leader that will remember that process for the rest of their life. Not all of them will pick it up at the same rate, and some won't know that was your intent. But when it happens, it will be one of the most gratifying moments you'll have as a leader. The bottom line is, don't be discouraged by people bringing you their problems—that's why you exist. Not only to make decisions but to make the right decisions. And not only to make the right decisions but to teach your subordinates why they were the right decisions. Better yet, you'll learn things about your people that you would have never known otherwise and you'll be humbled by how educated, intelligent and professional your subordinates are. You'll only know that by listening and empowering them to take ownership of problems.

For leaders to synergize the art and science of leadership, they must know who they work for and who they work with. Countless times, I have observed people get this wrong. For some mentally or emotionally weak reason, some people believe that leaders work *with* their subordinates and *for* their superiors. If you believe this, you are a boss or are aspiring to be a boss. True leaders work *for* their subordinates and *with* their superiors. In any industry in the world, people are the most important aspect of everything. Every single organization in the world has a customer, regardless of if it is a for-profit or nonprofit. If you're in the military or business or an athletic coach, you have a customer. If you're a leader, your direct and most important customers are your subordinates. Your purpose is to resource your customers. You resource them—most importantly with your time and effort. Sometimes they will need to be resourced with reality, perspective and corrective action, but it's your responsibility and duty to deliver for your customer.

How many times have you seen leaders work tirelessly on a project for their superiors only for it to fail or be completely unsupported by those who actually have to utilize it? Now ask yourself, how many times has a subordinate brought you an issue and a recommended solution that you endorsed, supported, and watched flourish? Someone that experiences this specific problem every single day (which likely means they aren't the only one experiencing it) trusts you enough to identify a problem and offer you a way to fix it. You provide that subordinate the time required to gain a shared understanding, inform your superiors of what your team is working on (which requires zero decision making or brain cells from them). The team executes it, and it works. What you just did is empower your team to fix a self-identified issue, allow let them own it and watch them celebrate a success. That is a customer experience that will remain for as long as you will allow it.

Leaders work with superiors by understanding, owning and distributing leader intent. Which makes their intent your intent, and in turn it becomes your subordinates' intent. The customer of that intent is the subordinates. You work with your superiors by being the leader willing to deliver bad news when it's necessary. Bosses are scared of this and use their "work for" mentality to blame their superiors for information that's hard to deliver to a customer. Working with your superiors allows your subordinates to advocate for you when you're not present. Because your subordinates know you will always work for them, the feedback they will provide to your superiors about your performance will speak volumes—more than if you were to work for your superiors. Take a break and read that again. I know the number of mentions of subordinates and superiors were excessive, but it's worth understanding.

CHARACTER

True leaders apply their leadership values into any position. A leader's values are grounded in their character. Character is the foundation in which all other leadership attributes and competencies are built upon. If a leader's character is weak, it will be exposed in times of difficulty, stress, and extremes. This is when leadership counts. When everything is falling around you, do you have the intestinal fortitude to do what is right versus what may be easy? This must be done regardless of the repercussion or perception. The first indication that an aspiring leader lacks or requires development in their character is if they lead by the position they fill. This is a common mistake I have observed in aspiring or eager leaders, regardless of rank, position or age. Sometimes aspiring leaders formulate a mental image of what they believe the position requires and therefore act in a manner they believe fits the position. This is a recipe for failure because your true character, good, bad or indifferent, will always prevail when truly challenged. Those who knew you before you took this position will quickly identify that you are attempting to lead, based on your assumptions about the position versus executing the leadership fundamentals that likely landed you the position. I have observed this in newly appointed commanders in the military, recently nominated captains in athletics and recently promoted bosses in the business world. Individuals who lead by position, although well-intentioned, have failed to conduct the proper assessment of their position and organization—but most of all, they failed to find the role the organization needed them to fill.

True leaders take their time to assess climate, culture and individual and team performance as well as critically think about what the organization needs from them in order to be successful. Most leaders I see struggling consistently ask themselves what they, as an individual, need to do to be successful, instead of asking themselves what role the organization needs them to fill to make the organization successful.

The highest performing leaders have the ability to look at themselves and their organization from different angles and elevations to identify issues, performance, and reality. Bruce Lee was a master of this when describing the importance of becoming like water. This applies perfectly to leadership regardless of position or industry. The human dimension of leadership means that no position or team will ever be the same over time because their leaders change, and people differ. This is why it's dangerous to provide overarching leadership guidance or requirements based on position. However, if we apply the water method to leadership, we can maintain a foundational constant while adapting to our environment and serving the people we work with and for.

If a leader attempts to be like water, their molecular formula remains the same. Water's foundation of two hydrogen atoms and one oxygen atom should be analogous with a leader's values, morals, and ethics. Regardless of whether water is required by the environment to be a gas, liquid or solid, its molecular foundation stays the same. A high performing leader shows the same ability by applying their foundational character into consistently changing leadership environments. Water is required to change its form based on temperature, like a leader is required to change their approach based on the organizational climate. Water vapor or gas rises during evaporation or during the application of heat, much like leaders should rise above heated and contentious issues in the workplace such as politics, sexual orientation or religion. Liquid water is a transparent, odorless and colorless substance with the ability to form to whatever figure is necessary. True leaders are also transparent with their intent, guidance, and weaknesses. They lead colorlessly by remaining consistent in their servanthood and customer service regardless of the demographics of the people they lead and serve. Water is the single most important constituent to life, as people are the single most important constituent to leaders. Solid water, or ice, regulates temperature, is hard and has the strength to cut through the planet's most difficult terrain. Leaders ensure solidarity in the team, control their emotions when people become heated and make hard decisions that change the work environment.

AWARENESS

A leader's awareness is vital to accurately assessing situations. After character, awareness is the next foundational layer to true leadership. Without awareness, leaders are unable to accurately perceive at any level. Awareness consists of self-awareness, team awareness, and organizational awareness. Leaders who are consistently aware are master observers; their attention to detail is remarkable. They can identify the most minor differences in their people if they are having a good or bad day, which allows them to be empathically aggressive and to positively meddle in the lives of their people. If some leaders contain this observational skill in the lives of others, think about how aware they are of themselves. Have you observed a leader make a decision and knew immediately that it was a terrible one? Or listen to someone talk about their high performance when every single person around them knows that the person couldn't be more wrong? It's incredible to see how some people manipulate or self-manifest their actions to highlight themselves instead of actively seeking ways to improve. This is a complete lack of self-awareness. Sometimes this happens when we only focus on our strengths and not our weaknesses. Some Fortune 500 companies openly advertise that they only focus on their leaders' strengths in the attempt to overpower their weaknesses. This is an awful methodology. Individuals and organizations need to be able to provide candid feedback to themselves and others in order to know their weaknesses, acknowledge them and attempt to improve them. This will result in awareness.

Although I didn't realize it until later in life, I was taught awareness at an early age. My parents would describe this to me in small but meaningful ways, such as the perception of our family based on how we behaved in a store or at church. I distinctly remember being briefed and warned about how I was to act in a public place and the repercussions if I didn't. My parents would also point out the good and mostly bad examples of behavior or conduct to ensure I understood the expectation, and what it looked like. These lessons resonated deeper and longer whenever pain accessorized the conversation. Don't confuse my words—I'm not saying my brother and I were beaten or abused by my parents. But I am saying that the bottom-line reality of life, regardless of culture, religion or country is that violence gets results. Period. For example, being told to stop yelling on the way to church, to which we would stop for about thirty seconds, would result in either my mother turning around with bright red nails and pinching you as though you offered your most sensitive flesh to a 20lb lobster claw or my father reaching behind the driver's seat with, what to me looked like a grizzly paw, squeezing my knee to the point where

I thought my leg snapped—both of which teach you the right answer before a nice talking to does. Like most children, I learned (and still learn) through repetition and failure. Every time I failed to follow simple instructions, there was a repercussion. That resulted in my perceived, uncanny ability to observe. Later, as an athlete, I learned how my actions or lack thereof would affect the rest of the team. This is another reason I believe team sports are a significant contributing factor to leader development. They educate young people about the importance of contributing to something bigger than themselves and also teaches the importance of finding a role.

Actively seeking, finding and filling a role is a leader's responsibility. Identifying a role requires maturity, honesty, and awareness. Serving with great leaders has shown me that sometimes they are unrecognizable to others based on what the organization required of them at the time. Leaders who have mastered the ability to find a role are perceived differently by those they have worked with in the past. Multiple times I have run into peers who have served with a specific great leader and while comparing stories, I learned that our experiences were completely different. One peer would tell a story about how funny and approachable this leader was, and the other peer, while saying he never observed that, did tell stories about how individually competent that same leader was. This variation resonated with me as a young leader. To me, it meant that leaders must contain a foundational leadership ability, and if talented enough, can change (like water) the form they take based on the requirements of their organization or mission. This is organizational awareness. These leaders knew that the organization was perceived a certain way and therefore molded their individual leadership ability to ensure the highest possible performance for the organization.

Leaders should know how they are perceived by their peers, their subordinates and their superiors. They should be humble and unbiased enough to reenact their performance and peel it back with amazing detail. Leaders should be their own worst critic. Without emotion, they should be able to evaluate their own performance as if they were a complete stranger and a spectator to it. How do others perceive you? How do you perceive yourself? With that said, you don't know what you don't know. So, I understand it would be difficult for a leader with no self-awareness to self-assess. To confirm or deny your self-awareness, ask someone you know will shoot you straight. Not your parents, or sometimes not your spouse. Ask someone who you know doesn't like you. Have the courage to hear something that you probably already know, but are too scared to admit that others are aware of. Ask your subordinates, and trust me, based on your industry, they are dying to tell you something about you that you don't know. Think of the benefits. You humble yourself; you toughen yourself; you show others your genuine interest to improve and show others you care about their opinion. Blatantly ask your boss. It will force them to provide you with feedback that may be holding you back or force them to substantiate whatever opinion they have of you.

INTERPERSONAL SKILL

If you have the courage to approach someone you know doesn't think highly of you, you probably have interpersonal skills.

Interpersonal skill is the ability to effectively communicate and relate to people. To take it one step further, I believe true interpersonal skill is the ability to effectively communicate and influence people anywhere on the socioeconomic spectrum. Leaders with high emotional intelligence or interpersonal skill have an extremely rare ability to maintain a conversation with anyone from a blue-collar laborer to a white-collar lawyer and make them feel valued.

I have always considered interpersonal skills an intangible leadership quality because it's almost impossible to teach in adulthood. Which is why a leader with interpersonal skill or a high emotional intelligence is what truly distinguishes them from their peers. This leader can completely balance the art and science of leadership. They can seamlessly scale their conversation to the recipient's level without being offensive or out of their league. Having interpersonal skills makes you approachable and relatable. Think about the importance of leading operations in a Fortune 500 company that consists of primarily low paid, low-skilled laborers and communicating the intent of its CEO. Think about how difficult or challenging it is for a leader with no interpersonal skills to explain a Fortune 500 CEO's intent to that company's lowest-paid employee. Conversely, think about how difficult or challenging it is for that same leader to explain the perspective of the lowest-paid employee to that Fortune 500 CEO. Imagine leading one of the largest, most culturally diverse organizations in the world whose mission or task can result in the death of its members or others without interpersonal skill.

You gain interpersonal skills by being a life-long learner in as many topics as humanly possible—from learning a trade to financial planning, from learning how to change your oil to practicing yoga and meditation. The more you are willing to branch out from your own comfortability, the greater the likelihood that you'll develop lasting relationships. You will be surprised how much you learn about yourself and people. You'll learn some of the most miserable people in the world have the most material assets, money, authority and "education." And some of the happiest people in the world are the poorest, but they value and appreciate their family, their trade or job and being alive more than anyone else. Parents, teachers, and coaches of our young people are the leaders that cultivate interpersonal skill. They should be doing this by exposure—sometimes forced exposure. Exposing adolescents to reality and working Americans' perspective is how interpersonal skill is conditioned. How do children of wildly successful families or parents teach their children to be leaders? This is a difficult question. I am sure we all know of parents who grew up with close to nothing, were forced to work for literally every single thing that they had, and grew up to be wildly successful. How does the individual that grew up in that scenario, who is now living a life of privilege, teach their children the value of truly hard work when the environment they are raising their children in is fundamentally different and easier than their childhood?

My honest answer is I have no idea, because I cannot relate to being wildly successful, but I can certainly say that my children have already been provided with more than I ever had. However, I would recommend two forms of exposure that will likely result in interpersonal skills and emotional intelligence. First, make them learn a trade when they are old enough to work. They won't appreciate the value of experience until they are older but think about the developmental opportunity. The skill and labor alone are value enough, but more than that, think about the stories and life experiences they will hear while working in this trade. They will experience the full gamut of life successes and total failure of drug addicts, prisoners and the formally uneducated. Next, make them volunteer or "voluntell" them to an organization or mission that is bigger than themselves. The bottom line is exposure to the less fortunate will humble the malleable mind to strive to be an interpersonal leader.

HUMILITY

Humility is acknowledging that you have something to learn from anyone and everyone, regardless of age or position. As a leader, you will find that as you progress through the ranks, you magically become smarter and funnier. If you spend long enough in any career path or industry, and you realize you are magically becoming the smartest and funniest person in the room, it just means you're the highest-ranking person or yield some type of decision-making authority over the rest of group—that's it. The reality is, as you progress in your career you make more mistakes and therefore learn more from them. It's not your intellect, it's you becoming wise and experienced. Leaders should periodically remind themselves of their mistakes to ensure they remain grounded in their roles. Think about that every time an eager, young leader has spent hours or days mulling over an idea that has already been attempted and never really worked out. Have the humility to hear them out to observe their thought process and attention to detail.

True leaders present their weaknesses openly and share the lessons learned from their past mistakes with their subordinates. It will remind them that you're human. Humility also means not taking yourself too seriously. If you're married, and you happen to be a senior leader, you likely understand that you're not in charge once you get home. Most people, regardless of socioeconomic status, can relate to that. I believe that injecting humor into your role as a leader is critical to your approachability and ultimately, establishing cohesion amongst the team. Much like art or music, humor is emotionally powerful and can be used to completely disarm or deflate otherwise terrible situations. Anyone who thinks there is no room for vulgarity or wit in leadership has never worn a tool belt, been punched in the face, jumped out of an aircraft or been in a locker room. Language is amazing to me; words are important, all of which have meaning. They describe feelings, contain and display emotions and carry emphasis. Any medium that has the power to completely change someone's emotions or state of influence should not be undervalued or go unutilized by leaders. There is definitely a time and a place for vulgarity and humor in any industry or position. The ability to remove whatever topic is weighing on your subordinate, even for just a moment to make them feel more comfortable, is worth it. Think about the gravity and seriousness of the situations we put our subordinates through. Most will never really know true pressure, but we all feel some sort of pressure to perform. Our wellbeing depends on it. Some of our nation's junior leaders are directly responsible for the life and death of many others. That honor and immense responsibility are not lost on them. So, any time that we can alleviate that stress will ensure a better product.

I remember taking a position in an organization that at the time suffered from extremely low morale, burn out and fatigue. I noticed fundamental issues in individual and collective performance that required a lot of change. Instead of providing the reality of the team's low performance and the changes I planned to implement, I deliberately decided that the team and the organization required that I fulfill a jovial, witty role. I acknowledged that at times, this would cost me credibility with my superiors and in some cases, I knew I was putting my reputation at risk. However, I was able to make the mundane and the difficult more palatable with wit, humor, and honesty. When something sucked to complete, I told the team I thought it was going to suck, but needed to be done and why. When I made mistakes, I openly made fun of myself to show my subordinates I was vulnerable. I openly asked for their help, even if I didn't truly need it, to give them ownership of their leader's development. I would poke fun at my team to my leaders, to illuminate our thought process and to show we were human. I highlighted the performance of my team, down to the individual, so my superiors would recognize them as they passed each other in the hall. We were able to ensure the team was running efficiently, in a gear that was sustainable and light. Over time, this technique also highlighted our contribution when things needed to be serious. When laughing and joking wasn't appropriate, we were able to quickly shift gears and perform better than other teams because we understood the significance of failure. Real failure, like people dying failure. We performed better than other teams, sections or elements because I coached them to understand the difference between a time to learn and laugh, and a time to exceed expectations for the greater good. This resulted in unquestioned loyalty, talent retention and credibility that other sections just did not have.

Think about what is to be gained with humility and humor in leadership. I guarantee that if you make humility a leadership priority, you will learn more about your organization than you would have thought possible. The comfortability of your leaders to speak truth to power is something you control. I have observed leaders who are incapable of doing this well, and it results in walls being placed around known friction points and problems. When people become afraid to deliver bad news to their superiors or violate their integrity to tell the boss what he wants to hear, it results in the organization becoming mediocre. I have observed professional leaders make up answers just to have an answer versus having the backbone to say "I don't know." My advice to aspiring leaders is always openly acknowledged that you don't know something. Now, don't confuse this recommendation. If there is something that you know you should know, you are on your own and should take full responsibility. However, you are going to be asked the most difficult questions by your leaders. Questions you can't rehearse for. If you don't know the answer, your professional response should be "I don't know, I need to think about it a bit longer, and I will get back to you" or "I don't know, but I will find out and get you the answer before you leave today." It shows that you are genuinely interested in the right answer or that you will do everything within your span of control or influence to get that answer.

Listening is another pillar of humility. The easiest way to display your freedom from pride or arrogance is to shut up and listen. This is harder for some than you might think. There is nothing worse than looking at a superior while presenting information to them, knowing they are just waiting for you to be finished speaking in order to swarm you with "guidance" or their perspective. Observant people can immediately identify that a person is not interested in what they are being told. They notice by a lack of eye contact, body language, and other nonverbal cues. Native Americans, for example, were wildly misunderstood in this regard. From an early age, they were deliberately taught that silence is a cornerstone of character. You were not to speak until you had something truly meaningful to contribute, and you were confident that no other person was speaking. We would be smart to integrate this practice of respect in all that we do, but I fear that our ever-increasing compilations of statistical meaninglessness overwhelm our ability to listen to one another.

I once joined a small team of senior leaders in a discussion about workplace safety in which fourteen total people participated—four leaders and ten employees. The conversation intended to determine if the employees felt they worked in a safe environment, and we had about sixty minutes to complete this discussion. For fifty-three minutes, I observed two of the four senior leaders talk at the ten employees. I was in shock of what I was watching unfold. In a last-minute effort to advocate for the employees, I injected myself into the conversation and asked that we simply go around the table to hear from each employee. The eagerness with which the employees entered the room simply died over the fifty-three minutes and their submissions were clearly shorter because they were offended by what had ensued. After the meeting, one of the senior leaders pulled me aside and asked what I thought. I said, "I thought it was awful, we just spoke at them for over fifty minutes." A bit taken back, he looked at me and said: "Listen (which I thought was funny), be careful about allowing them the opportunity to complain, it becomes contagious and the other employees may agree if they hear it." I gave no response because it goes against absolutely everything that I had been taught as a leader of people. The leader that said this had absolutely no malicious intent with his comment, but he simply never had been taught and shown the right way to lead people.

The leader responsible for this task should have dominated the details of the event. Deliberately choose employees that will make the conversation meaningful and honest. Ensure the meeting isn't held at a time that would hinder the conversation, such as during their lunch hour or at the end of the day. Anticipate questions and responses and be prepared to represent the company and its leaders in a positive light. Ensure that the majority of the time used for the meeting is given to the employees to speak. They have likely been waiting a long time to get the opportunity to speak their mind to a leader or leaders. Remember, they usually don't have the access to speak with you, as you do with them. When they speak to you, attempt to empathize and relate to their perspective. Repeat their issue back to them. Make sure they know that you are listening. Give them your undivided attention. Take notes and provide some type of feedback for action such as "so if I understand you correctly, you're saying… (insert X comment) and it's affecting you this way, is that correct?" I have found, that leaders sometimes trap themselves by either making a promise they can't keep or making such a quick recommendation without truly weighing the options that the employee is almost offended. They become offended because your response is sometimes so fundamental that it implies the employee wasn't intelligent enough to think of it themselves. The leader should tell the employee what their next steps will be to rectify the issue at hand. "I will speak to X person or people who may provide some historical knowledge on the issue and let you know how it develops so you're aware of any changes that may affect your work, and I will get back to you no later than X date to let you know what headway I have made." The final and most important aspect of this entire interaction is the follow-up. If you don't follow up, you've lost all credibility. The employee likely doesn't know, or maybe even care, how much you have on your plate, but that's what you're paid to do. When you follow up, regardless of the outcome of your research, you have to make them aware that it was their ownership of the issue that resulted in a positive change. If in your research you learn why something was happening a certain way and the process cannot be changed, you owe them that feedback too. They will genuinely understand and appreciate that you took the time to resolve their issue and it will resonate with them.

WORK ETHIC

The intrinsic motivation to get results is driven by a leader's work ethic. This intangible attribute is usually seen in leaders who have endured struggle and challenge early in life. We all know individuals with incredible stories of perseverance—from individuals arriving in America within no money, family or understanding of the language, to people who risk everything they have to start, sustain and profit in business. The American dream is possible through an unparalleled work ethic. Leaders who have and maintain an unmatched work ethic are simply hard not to follow. These leaders gain followership and support through their example. Work ethic is strong enough to compensate for natural ability and talent. I would argue that people are more apt to follow and support lower talent, high work ethic leaders than leaders with high talent and low work ethic. Everyone can relate to the determination and drive associated with work ethic. We have seen films and read books that highlight the underdog who is required to work longer and harder than everyone else to maintain on equal level with his peers. The bottom line about work ethic was provided to us by Benjamin Franklin when he said: "Better well done, then well said." Leaders influence people to achieve results, and they do that by never asking their subordinates to do something they are not willing to do themselves. A leader's work ethic is what drives them to understand. Understanding what their subordinates experience, and understanding themselves in times of extreme stress. The byproduct of a great work ethic is learning more about your limits. When you exert the energy, time and due diligence that a leader should, you find out exactly what your limits are. And if you have learned what your limit is, you are more likely to accurately assess the work ethic of others.

It's not hard to work hard. I would argue that it is easier than not working hard. Being lazy and looking for ways to not work hard is harder than just working hard. You expend more energy in finding ways not to work hard than if you were to just work hard. When you work hard, your subordinates will notice and most will think "If he can do it, then I can do it." That's influence and it costs you, as the leader, nothing. With that said, experience will allow you to choose when to work hard and when to work smart. The all-too-familiar phrases we hear like "Work smarter, not harder," "There are smart Rangers and there are hard Rangers, and if you're not smart, then you better be hard," "Measure twice, cut once," and "We do it nice because we do it twice." These are all ways of saying that working smarter is better than working harder. However, there is no reason why leaders cannot facilitate both. Once you have learned a better, more efficient way to complete a task, you can then re-apply hard work to smart work. Once this occurs, your performance, and therefore the performance of your team, will increase. This will also make it easier to observe those who haven't assimilated because their peers will begin to outperform them.

There is a direct correlation between a leaders' work ethic and individual discipline. Leaders must have an individual discipline that allows them to lead with integrity. It will determine if a leader chooses the hard right versus the easy wrong. There are endless scenarios in which this will be tested. If there is nothing else that you take away from this section/chapter, it should be that "Joe is always watching." I have observed people in leadership positions violate their integrity or the integrity of their organization because it was easier than telling the truth or delivering bad news. This will eat away at you in the long run and I would argue that you probably undervalue the number of people, in particular your subordinates, that will know. "Joe is always watching" means that your subordinates/employees are always watching what you do and how you react. Not just when you speak, but every single thing that you do. Every action is noted and saved. Remember that perception is reality until proven otherwise, and first impressions are lasting. What you wear, who you choose to associate with both in and out of work, what and how you drive, what and how you eat—all of it. The employees or subordinates who are unable to spend a considerable amount of time with you due to your schedule, geographic location, etc. will judge you based on the above. So make the conscious decision every morning to remind yourself of that. That is not to say you should change who you are, because if you are pretending, that will be seen and known before you are aware of it. Examples of individual discipline range from email and correspondence etiquette, picking up trash or walking past it, grooming standard compliance, and actions you take when met with adversity. If you have an above-average worth ethic and individual discipline, you are likely adaptable and resilient.

How do you respond to rapidly changing circumstances? When your environment changes, will you have the composure and leadership presence that people gravitate towards? If so, you'll notice people will come to you for guidance and assurance that things will work out. In reality, you will likely have no real idea what the second and third-order effects are when a truly drastic change happens, but it is a leader's responsibility to compile the necessary information on either side of the change and turn that information into analyzed information. This is also known as intelligence. We should first understand that an original plan rarely unfolds the way we think it will, which is why short term, mid-term and long-term planning is so important. A leader should be able to envision contingencies, branches or sequels within a plan. If a leader is constantly stuck in the short term, they will be surprised constantly, which is a terrible way to feel while in any leadership position. Once you acknowledge that change is inevitable you will be better prepared to adapt to your environment. Your ability to maintain your composure, patience, and professionalism in changing circumstances will inform your subordinates and leaders of your reliability. Can you be trusted to lead when things get truly hard? General (ret.) and former Secretary of Defense James "Mad Dog" Mattis spoke of adaptability when he said: "Be polite, be professional, but have a plan to kill everybody you meet." I know that seems barbaric, but I assess that quote to mean things are going to change and are you going to be ready. Readiness implies preparation, and if you're adaptable, you have deliberately thought about the required actions, both above you and below you, when circumstances change. Resilient leaders can bounce back from adversity. Leaders are the people who look for opportunities in adversity. They view adversity as a way to test their people, their leadership skills and take meticulous note of their people's reactions as it will create an understanding of how people need to be trained and will react and perform under pressure in the future.

I once had the honor and privilege to be part of a very small group of leaders to talk to then-Secretary Mattis about the changing environment and what it meant for the organization I represented. I was in awe of his patience and composure given the seriousness of our discussion. When asked what kept him up at night, he simply chuckled and said: "Nothing. I keep others up at night." During that very discussion, a Mad Dog staffer came into the room and handed the Sec Def a piece of paper. He showed zero emotion when seeing the content of the paper. He simply nodded his head to show he understood and thanked the staffer. I later heard a rumor that the notification contained word that the Secretary of State at the time, Rex Tillerson was fired, and the note from the staffer was to notify the Sec Def. Candidly, I have no way to verify if this rumor is accurate in any way, but to be honest, it added to my already existing respect of this inherent leader. I remember thinking deliberately about how the information didn't sway his focus on us in the slightest. He continued discussing the most serious of topics with us, encouraging us to maintain a moral and tactical ethic and expressing how impressed he was with our continuous performance and leadership. Even if the above note-passing story is not true, I think about how I have observed other leaders or bosses respond to the news given to them in real-time. I can vividly remember the first "leader" meeting I attended after I left the Army. During this meeting, which happened to be about safety, an employee burst into the room to inform the company leaders that a safety incident just occurred and someone had gotten hurt. I watched in disbelief as the senior leader of our organization immediately got up and essentially ran out of the room to investigate. I was floored by the knee jerk response that essentially ended the meeting. I immediately reverted to our discussion with Sec Def and how he responded to news that was more vital to more Americans than the one I had just encountered. I also thought about how many times I stood inches away from a senior leader when they were informed in real-time that one of their men was seriously wounded or killed in action. I remembered them being notified in person or over the radio, while they were patiently raising a cup of hot coffee before a sip. I remembered how they received the terrible news as they began and completed their sip of the coffee without breaking the slightest of movement. How by the time the cup was lowered and removed from their mouth, as if the news they were receiving was about the score of a sporting event, they acknowledged receipt of the information and guided the leader presenting the information if it was required.

I remembered how steady their hands were while they prepared to call the mother or father of a service member and watched them walk to a private place to deliver a parent's worst nightmare. I remember how these leaders would return from the call with their heads held high, remaining as mentally and emotionally present as they were before being notified. I watched as these leaders guided us through adversity while operations were still being conducted because they appreciated that a mission still needed to be met and that winning was important. There were still many men in harm's way and I observed how their decision-making ability didn't waver in the slightest due to the loss. If you ever wonder why leaders of this caliber look thirty years older than their actual age...this is why. They carry an unbelievable amount of grief, responsibility, and ownership. I didn't truly appreciate the composure, adaptability, and resiliency of these leaders until the moment I sat in my first business meeting.

Recently, I was traveling overseas when I was notified that one of my junior Rangers had stepped on an IED and lost his leg below the knee. Oddly enough, I had just spoken with this Ranger's father the day prior, before we departed the continental United States. Based on the nature of my travel, I had an extremely limited ability to contact his family, or anyone for that matter, for more information. My peers, subordinate leaders, and superiors quickly and calmly adjusted to the situation to ensure his family was properly notified, that medical care was provided and logistical preparations were made to ensure his safe return to the United States. He was successfully transported to Walter Reed Medical Center. This Ranger spent Thanksgiving at Walter Reed, and around 1000 that day, the Secretary of Defense, James Mattis walked into his room, alone. Completely by himself. The Walter Reed staff attempted to advise Mad Dog that his staff should have advised them of his visit. Mad Dog quickly interrupted and said he wasn't here to make a scene and that he was here to see this Ranger. Mad Dog and my Ranger spoke for around 30 minutes, just the two of them. When Mad Dog asked how he was doing, my Ranger quickly responded with "They may have changed the way I look. But not who I am." This is after he wrote, "Not today ISIS" soon after the blast and before going into one of his many surgeries.

He later thanked Secretary Mattis for his leadership and told him the guys knew he was probably in the middle of some incredibility difficult times. My Ranger let him know that the boys would do anything he needed them to do. After my Ranger told me about his visitor and the discussion they had, I went home and cried to my wife about the importance of leadership and how impressed I was with such an act of true leadership. I thought about the gravity of responsibility the Sec Def had on his shoulders at the time he prioritized a visit to see this Ranger, on a national holiday. I thought about how at the time Yemen was on fire, many administration cabinet members and high-ranking officials were being fired or resigning, Brexit was occurring, Afghanistan had no end in sight, and we were closer to a full-scale conventional war with North Korea than people appreciated. These are the best examples that I will likely ever be able to provide regarding adaptability, resiliency, and how a leader responds to adversity.

People in leadership positions who are unable to adapt are likely afraid of failure. Leaders are responsible for defining both success and failure because they are both so vague and subjective. Leaders that fail to define success and failure hinder the development and operability of their subordinates. When employees or subordinates are unclear on what you define success to be, they will develop their own definitions—which could be drastically different from your intent or desired end state. It's logical and necessary to assume that different jobs, occupations or professions view failure very differently. I would submit that the only time when failure should not be accepted, encouraged and reinforced is when it results in the death of people. For example, when it is decided to go to war, it's important that we win because if we fail, our service members die and our national interests are put at risk. However, if we work for a Fortune 500 company, failure is required to innovate, make technological discoveries and improve. This is what I mean when I say failure is subjective. Because 99% of Americans cannot relate to real failure, leaders in the business world should be willing to accept failure as a learning tool. As I have stated earlier in this book, good judgment usually stems from previous poor judgment. For most people to truly learn, they must attempt something and fail to learn how to succeed at it later. Leaders unwilling to fail generally ask permission for everything instead of asking for forgiveness if things don't go as planned. Leaders should instill trust in their subordinates to make decisions without their direct oversight. Leaders who develop their subordinates to act and make informed decisions without fear of mistakes or failure will cultivate a culture of disciplined initiative and discretion that will represent your organization well.

MENTAL TOUGHNESS

The culmination of work ethic, discipline, readiness, adaptability, and resiliency is mental toughness. Any professional athlete, combat operator or top business executive would likely agree that the common denominator of highly successful people is their mindful grit. They are so conscious of their own being that they can simply apply their mind and body to an objective and achieve it. Leaders with this attribute can achieve what they choose. They merely have to convince themselves that it's humanly possible. The easiest way to observe a leader's potential mindfulness and grit is through their physical performance.

Leaders who do this well have trained their mind to turn off pain, sleep deprivation, hunger, and fatigue. All humans can do this and occasionally, we catch glimpses of it in times of complete hysteria or extremis, such as when a parent displays a feat of extreme strength by lifting a vehicle off of a child in a life-and-death scenario. Our minds are capable of doing things that I don't believe we truly understand yet. I am not saying that leaders need to be superhuman to influence people, but I am saying that leaders have an unbelievable ability or potential to achieve whatever they choose, and they can do it because of mental toughness. I also believe that being mindfully gritty is trainable. It's not genetically predisposed to any one type of person. All of us have the potential to expose it. Recent studies of consciousness and mindfulness have shown us that deliberate concentration and meditation have significantly positive effects regarding human performance, healing, and wellness. When most people think of meditation, they think of monks or yogis attempting to achieve a level of consciousness that isn't fully accepted in the western world yet. But I would offer that all people—especially leaders—should make a time investment in their mental toughness and consciousness. At a more understandable level, athletes and operators have all spent time envisioning their performance, endlessly rehearsing their actions in their minds to make it a reality. This takes practice, and then more practice.

Making a time investment in the practice of mindfulness will refine our mental toughness. Because leaders tend to enjoy preparation and readiness, they are able to exercise this activity in order to improve their proficiency. There is no debating the causality between practice and performance. This is why leaders advertise things like "practice how you play" and "the more you sweat in training, the less you bleed in war." When your body, mind, and senses are presented with a fight-or-flight scenario, you will resort to the muscle memory your mind has put your body through, and it will respond, almost automatically. Although your brain isn't a muscle, but an impressive symmetrical array of gray and white matter and cellular structure, it controls your bodily response. If this is a fact, then mental toughness and mindfulness are trainable and observable.

The best leaders attempt to train their minds as much as their bodies. The relationship between your mind and your body ought to be symmetrical. Leaders who focus too much on one area become lopsided and fall short when challenged in the realm that they didn't train or keep practiced. As a complete leader, it is not enough to be the smartest person in the room or the fittest person in the room. Those things alone are completely meaningless in leadership. The reason why balancing cognitive ability and physical ability is important is because you are charged with influencing and leading a diverse group of people and they deserve to be led by a physically capable, cognitively developed leader. Leaders should have an insatiable appetite to improve themselves and can only dedicate themselves to improve through mental toughness.

I would recommend that leaders attempting to become mentally tough should first become physically tough. It's the easiest way to gauge your mental toughness. If you find yourself quitting or giving up on your pursuit of physical toughness, it's because you're mentally weak. Our bodies are, without question, capable of amazing feats, which means *your* body is no different. Your body is stopping because your mind is convincing itself, and therefore your body, that it can't continue. Develop achievable, realistic physical goals that your mind is willing to uphold. Over time and with practice, you will establish physical toughness, which will, in turn, yield mental toughness. Your body will naturally introduce you to levels of increased training through pain. Pain is good—it's an indicator of locations in your body where you can apply your mind. When in pain, some people say "mind over matter, and if you don't mind, then it don't matter." Some folks say "stop thinking about it and it'll go away." These are very easy ways of explaining a more complex process of how your mind controls your body. Leaders should make every attempt to be as complete as possible. "The Nation that makes a great distinction between its scholars and its warriors will have its thinking done by cowards and its fighting done by fools." Greek philosopher Thucydides was referring to the criticality of being as complete as possible.

CRITICAL THINKING

Do you have the discipline to remove bias from your thought process? Leaders actively question their thinking and look for ways to disprove themselves. I once heard Jeff Bezos speak about the importance of bringing a "beginner's mind" to an area of perceived expertise. This is brilliant. Leaders should attempt to remove themselves from their perceived understanding of an issue, area or topic and reattack it as if it's the first time they've been exposed to it. I understand that this is much easier said than done. I imagine this is why successful companies actively pursue external leaders. How many times have you watched yourself mull over a genuinely difficult issue and hit roadblock after roadblock, only to see a talented individual with no experience in the field or topic make a valuable contribution or suggestion after minutes of hearing the problem? After the self-loathing and disappointment subsides, you realize this happens because the person was able to see the problem from a completely different vantage point. Leaders are at least aware of their own biases and can critically critique their own thought process, which is why true leaders seek the opinions and perspectives of others. Attempting to remove your biases from your thought process is a difficult self-science. The art of critical thinking as a leader is understanding when and how to exercise your thought process. Leaders should be careful when "thinking out loud." In almost all cases, thinking out loud is healthy and beneficial. There is something to be said about briefing an argument or thought to yourself. Audibly receiving your own thought or argument is a rehearsal of how you would present the thought, which will, in turn, generate questions that may result. However, I have seen leaders conduct this process in front of subordinates and it go wrong. When leaders do not clearly communicate their thoughts or that they are just thinking out loud, subordinates will confuse those thoughts for guidance and will then expend individual and organizational energy in things that you had no intent for them to pursue.

For example, if you think out loud in a meeting of twenty people and you don't disclaim that you are thinking out loud for a moment, the law of averages tells us that at least a few subordinate leaders will confuse the out-loud thought for actionable guidance. This will, in turn, result in those subordinate leaders pursuing a course of action that you had no intent for them to pursue. One week, one month or maybe one quarter later, those subordinate leaders will return to you and brief you on their progression in an area that you never tasked them to look into or improve, and suddenly you'll realize the gravity of your position as a leader. You realize that the organizational energy of an entire group of people, which may require effort and action by tens of thousands of people, was driven by you thinking out loud for a matter of minutes. Now, apply this scenario to all levels of leadership and think about its potential effects. If a CEO of a Fortune 500 company or a General Officer does this, think about the amount of time, money and effort potentially wasted. The leadership lesson here is that words are important—communicate your thought process clearly and know that as a leader, critical thinking applies to everything… even thinking out loud.

MENTORSHIP AND COUNSELING

More than other aspects of being a leader, I enjoy the mentorship and counsel associated with developing leaders. The importance of mentorship in leadership is equivalent to the olfactory system in our senses. The olfactory system manages our sense of smell and is the oldest and longest-lasting of the senses. Mentorship is the legacy of a leader. I know the word legacy sounds a bit pretentious or extreme, but when you leave for a different position or company, or even when we die, the mentorship we provided will be what we leave behind. And as leaders, it's our responsibility to teach, coach and mentor developing leaders to maximize their potential, provide them a challenge and pass the lessons learned from our previous mistakes. You have to genuinely want other people to be successful.

Leadership counseling is the vehicle of mentorship. Providing counsel is when a leader facilitates an engaging, meaningful conversation with a developing leader. It is a two-way engagement to discuss barriers, challenges, performance, expectations, and goals of each other. Leaders should have an almost natural ability to make others feel comfortable enough to openly share both personal and professional goals. The importance of counseling and mentorship cannot be understated. It's one of the most imperative responsibilities of a leader. Leaders should make every attempt to refine their mentorship and counseling skills. They should make every effort to dominate every detail associated with counseling. We've established why counseling is important, but leaders should attempt to manage the what, when, where and how as well. As a leader, you can control the majority of these conditions, so when the operating environment allows you the time and space to control the counseling environment, we should take advantage. To me, the ideal counseling session looks like this (from the perspective of the mentor).

Prior: I provide the mentee a counseling document or statement that describes my vision, intent, guidance, and priorities. This document is clear, concise and two levels above my current position (Strategic, Operational, Tactical) to provide the mentee a frame of reference of what's expected of me, which will provide them a purposeful reference for what I am asking of them. I provide these documents no later than 24 hrs. in advance of our scheduled meeting. I inform the mentee that I expect them to read the documents in order to facilitate a conversation. I ensure that all support staff, subordinates, and counterparts are aware of my scheduled counseling time to ensure no distractions.

When: I schedule counseling at a time that ensures my attention is singularly focused. I stay away from scheduling sessions first thing in the morning. Allow people to settle into their day and set conditions to be successful. I also stay away from scheduling them directly after lunch and at the very end of the duty/business day. There is nothing worse than diving deep into a conversation directly after a meal—especially because it's impossible to be entirely sure how the conversation will go. The reason I don't schedule this type of meeting at the end of the day is that you don't want to be the final barrier between a person and their family. Nor should you expect their undivided attention and effort if they've been working hard all day. The frequency of counseling is dependent upon the type of counseling and type of organization you're in. I would argue that monthly counseling is the most ideal because it allows both you and the person your counseling the time to put into practice what was discussed in the previous session. It ensures that both of you remember the previous conversation as well. However, this may not be feasible based on geographic location, the number of people you lead, etc. So, make it point to counsel your people no less than once a quarter (or every three months). The quarterly model works well because it is aligned with the fiscal year, which usually means organizational change as well as budgeting and funding allocation. Lastly, just because the formal portion of counseling is conducted quarterly doesn't mean informal counseling doesn't occur much more frequently.

How: I recommend never counseling from behind a desk. Why would you? You are placing a physical barrier between you and the mentee. It detracts from the human element of a meaningful conversation. Whether you intend to or not, you're basically fostering a subservient situation where you are placing your position or rank above the person. I also ensure that my computer is closed and or off. There is nothing more disrespectful then openly answering emails while someone is telling you their personal and professional life goals. Leaders do this more than they would like to admit. If you think answering that email or checking a performance report is more important than the person you're talking to, who oddly enough, is one of the people contributing to the performance, then you're a boss, not a leader. And like anything else, you get what you put in. I do, however, keep my cell phone nearby on silent or vibrate. Life happens—don't be the leader that misses a family emergency. This will message to the mentee how seriously you take your role as a father, spouse, etc. Once these conditions are established, you can get to the purpose of the meeting. I always begin by giving a quick agenda of what we should accomplish in the meeting, which keeps both parties honest and on task. If the conversation goes well, it should be tough to cover all the topics you intended, because the conversation evolves, deepens and branches out. I usually follow the agenda with what they thought of the documents I provided them and then I listen more then I speak. Based on your position, think about how long a person has been waiting to share what they are sharing. Empathize with their position, and think about how many times you have been talked at. Allow them to reveal their thought process. You'll learn more about the person, the position, the organizational climate, and culture. It is okay to help the person through their story or explanation to get to a point. You should be coaching this aspiring leader on how to vocalize their thoughts and experiences.

What: What topics should you cover in a mentorship session? First, understand that the mentee has a vote as well. If they guide you to a topic of interest, let them. Nevertheless, I would always ensure the following was discussed before we ended the conversation.

Expectations of each other need to be addressed. Yes, it's incredibly valuable to hear from the people who work for you about what their expectations of you are. Some mentees will be at a loss for words when you ask them what you need to be better at. Ask them how you can help them do their job to the best of their ability. Ask them if they can provide you an example of a time they thought you should have done something differently. The person being counseled will genuinely appreciate that you are interested in their feedback. You'll be surprised by what you learn about that person and about yourself. Take notes, which shows them you are going to pursue whatever topics are mentioned. Remember, this is a two-way conversation. Never do anything with one purpose—if you do this right, you both get better based on the conversation. Also, make it a point to ensure they know what is expected of them. Reciprocate by explaining to them what you see both their role and your role to be. As a leader of people, you are a resource manager. You are to provide and resource your people with what they need (and sometimes want) to complete the mission you've charged them with. Provide clear examples of standard and above standard performance in the position so there is no confusion as to where you stand with performance measures. Discuss "black swan" or red-line issues, such as unsafe acts, harassment, lack of integrity, lack of work ethic or shirking responsibility as a leader.

It's also important to gain an appreciation for the mentee's home life, interests and family dynamic. Have you ever worked with or for a leader whom you have spoken to only a few times and somehow, he remembers your spouse's name or anniversary? It floors you. The amount of respect you will garner for attempting to learn about the person in the position versus just the position's performance is astounding. Learning and discussing these types of topics will provide a leader insight into why the person thinks and performs as they do. Have you ever overreacted in the correction of a subordinate or employee just to learn that a serious family issue or an emergency occurred? And the person was trying to balance this occurrence with your high standard and expectation? It makes you feel pretty tiny and petty, but it happens. We are all humans and when that happens, apologize and support. You're not above it. The most competent leaders know when they are wrong and openly admit it when it happens. Discussing family dynamics can be difficult. An observant leader will notice when something isn't right, which means you'll probably hear about it again—whether it be from the person, from their peers, on the news or from the police. But tough and revealing conversations are exactly how you develop lasting relationships because they establish trust. I promise you will be surprised by some of the things you hear. You will gain an incredible appreciation for how you were raised, the adversity people face, how lucky you are to have what you have and what people are capable of. When it is time to discuss these types of topics with an aspiring leader or subordinate, it's important to describe your thoughts on work-life balance. High performing people, especially the most competent leaders, have a difficult time with this because they become so consumed with leading others that sometimes they don't lead themselves. I would broach this issue by vocalizing how I self-identify. At the time, I was a Military Intelligence Officer in the Army, a Company Commander in the 75th Ranger Regiment, a father and a husband. After years of self-identifying in this way, I realized my own struggle. I struggled with being the intelligence professional I *wanted* to be, the leader I *should* have been, and the husband and father I *needed* to be. When you can self-actualize to your subordinates, it helps them gain perspective about what is important in life, not just what's important for their career. Helping them come to this realization is the entire purpose of mentorship.

No two counseling sessions will be the same. If they are, then you are the problem. People are different, so let the counseling session go where it needs to and adjust when necessary. During my second company command position, my First Sergeant (1SG) and I would meet with all of the new privates when they came to the company. It was amazing to see how young and impressionable these Rangers were. After a couple of initial counseling sessions, we decided to dive a bit deeper into their development because they were generally very nervous to be speaking with their First Sergeant and Commander and therefore would not divulge anything that would lead to a meaningful conversation. So, I called their parents.

I asked each new Ranger to provide a point of contact for their parents and asked if they were okay with me calling. Of course, there were zero objections. I can't express in words how rewarding, hilarious and enjoyable it was to speak with the parents of the people who served in my command. I knew that when 1SG and I started making these calls parents would immediately think that their son or daughter was in trouble or injured. That's because when a leader calls the family of a service member it is usually to deliver bad news, not good news. Therefore, we made a deliberate, pointed effort when calling to immediately introduce ourselves and then state that their

Ranger was perfectly healthy and fine. Once their nervousness and anxiety subsided, we described how we were just calling to make them aware that we were the leaders responsible for their children. We acknowledged our responsibility to take care of their children and we didn't take it lightly. We explained that we understood that their sons and daughters were likely keeping them in the dark and we told them what to expect from their Rangers. We thanked them for raising children resilient enough to serve their country in a time of war and explained to them the significance of the unit and team their children were on. 1SG and I gave them our cell phone numbers and told them to feel free to contact us with any questions. The responses, support, and gratitude that we received from the parents were incredible, and I'll never forget how rewarding those calls were. Some of which were simply hilarious. Think about how culturally diverse America is and then think of the culture and norms of different areas around the country. In sixty minutes, 1SG and I would hear things ranging from how their midwestern boy was always number one in everything and how the lord selected him to be a Ranger. Some parents had no idea that their son was even in the special operations community, let alone what their job was. We were even told to kick their kids' ass if they acted up, how whoopin' their ass taught them discipline, that we needed to give them more time off and how they intended to write their congressmen, etc. I loved that experience.

Where: There will be plenty of times when you will be unable to control the counseling environment; the actions of a subordinate leader may dictate it be conducted in real-time. With that being said, a leader should understand that they are providing counsel every time they speak. Based on the number of people you lead; leaders should seize any opportunity to talk with their people. Every single interaction a leader has is a counseling opportunity. Walking to and from different rooms, to and from parking lots, in a break room, etc. You should be willing to counsel anywhere and anytime. After leaving the Army, I was extremely interested in how the Fortune 500 business world conducted leader development, mentorship, and counseling. My first counseling experience was exactly what I thought it would be—in an office, with a desk between myself and the boss. The boss had a computer in front of him. I deliberately sat in the chair diagonally across from him instead of directly across from him to ensure I could see him in totality instead of just what his computer allowed. However, the conversation we had was meaningful. I could tell that he was genuinely interested in what I had to say and that he was interested in teaching me. Nevertheless, I could tell when he lost interest in the conversation, and I watched him revert to his computer whenever it would beep or ding. Therefore, I had already planned to change the environment for our second counseling session. Thirty to forty days after my first counseling session, I was back on the calendar. While walking down to his office, I took a deliberate look out the window and noticed the weather would facilitate a conversation outside. As he stood in his office doorway waiting for me to enter, I asked if it would be okay for us to walk around the building for the counseling session. He was taken aback. After a minute of silence, I presented the fact that we already spend around twelve hours a day inside a building, so we should get outside and enjoy the weather. To seal the deal, I also added that we could ensure that the building's exterior and the parking lot were safe for our employees. I could tell he was taken by surprise, but I appreciated his willingness to go with the flow. On our way out the door, he told his administrative assistant that if he didn't return in an hour, it was because an Army Ranger likely killed him. This light-hearted comment was in direct result of being taken out of his comfort zone. Whether he intended for me to recognize it or not, he was showing me that he was willing to listen to my recommendations and that he had researched my past. To me, that joke was the perfect indicator that the conversation to follow would be infinitely more engaging than if we were to do it from behind a desk again.

The second counseling session was significantly better and more rewarding than the first. I had his complete attention. The human dynamic of the conversation had drastically increased because we were simply walking together and having a candid, open conversation. Sometimes bosses or leaders feel as though they have a reputation to uphold or an image to present. It's easy for them to do that when they're in their element, like in an office surrounded by plaques of their accomplishments and even more so, behind a big desk. But when you take them out of that scenario and humanize the situation, people are more willing to show you who they really are versus the boss or leader they think they ought to be or pretend to be.

Post counseling: Just before ending the counseling session, I would repeat back the major topics discussed to ensure that I understood, but more importantly to show the other person that I was listening and that I plan to follow through and up. I would also schedule their next counseling session with them in front of me. This would allow me to acknowledge where we would both be around that time. The session you're ending right now might very well be the last time you have a detailed conversation with this person based on multiple circumstances, i.e. deployment, re-location, etc., so make sure to thank them for what they do. The final step is proper data management. How are you saving the conversation you just had? My recommendation would be both a digital and hard copy records. It will ensure you can access your actual notes, as well as maintain the documents while traveling, for example.

Time is the most critical element of counseling. Time is a leader's capital and people are a leader's investment. Therefore, by counseling, you are making an investment in the future and the betterment of your organization. Leaders always feel pressured to find time to counsel. Because we are driven by the tyranny of the present, leaders will often cancel counseling sessions or appointments. They do this because they can completely control the date and time of when counseling is conducted. It's much easier to cancel a one-on-one engagement than it is to cancel a recurring, battle rhythm meeting containing twenty plus people. Especially if the results of such a meeting drives change for the organization. However, as a leader, you are failing if you find yourself canceling counseling sessions. Period. When a subordinate or junior leader performs poorly or exercises a lapse of judgment, my first question is when was the last time this person was counseled? Think about the message you're sending when you cancel a counseling session. You're telling a subordinate leader that you deliberately searched your schedule and decided that of the day's events, a conversation with you was least important. You're telling that subordinate leader that it is okay to not counsel or mentor their developing leaders. You have just lost credibility and trust as a leader. There is no excuse for not making time for your leaders. With that said, life happens, so of course, there will be times when you will need to re-schedule things based on unforeseen events and conflicts, but a leader owes that subordinate an honest explanation. They know you are incredibly busy; they understand the gravity of your responsibility and they know that sometimes you are just unable to conduct what you have planned based on unseen circumstances.

COMMUNICATION

A leader's ability to communicate with others will determine how successful the individual and the collective will be. Yes, communication is that important. The ability to expressively communicate meaning in all forms—written, spoken and unspoken—is vital to influence and understanding. In my opinion, some people regress in their ability to communicate over time. This is because we allow preconceived notions, cultural and societal norms and assumptions to get in the way of effectively communicating. Think about the differences between how a baby communicates, how a child communicates and finally how most adults communicate. A baby's communication is instinctive and therefore highly effective. For the most part, when a baby communicates, they're either hungry or in pain. When children communicate, it's without filter. How many times have you witnessed a child's observation in a grocery store or a crowded restaurant "Hello, why are you so fat?" "Hey, mom, why do you hate daddy's mommy?" "This tastes like poop." In most cases, children speak in truths and have no qualms about it.

By adulthood, we pack our communication techniques with educational bias; we hide behind technology; we brag about how "we tell it like it is." The reality is, most people are scared of delivering and receiving candid feedback. Most adults attempt to speak or write in a way that represents who they think they are or who they want to be. People will purposely overcomplicate their words because they think sounding smart makes them smart, and they're hoping to impress the recipient. How about the person who takes five minutes to say something that could be effectively communicated in five seconds? When you're the recipient of this persons' communication, it's hard not to slowly put your index finger perpendicularly on their lips and say, in a completely controlled and patient voice "shut the fuck up, I got it."

The number of communication mediums available today makes it easy for us to hide behind our tech, but more importantly, we have forgotten how and why we communicate. There are three forms of communication that a leader should keep in contention and enforce. The primary communication method is face-to-face (f2f). When you communicate this way, each person acknowledges the topic at hand and the time spent to communicate it. When you use f2f, you can communicate with more than just your words. The recipient of the information can observe your body language and therefore can observe your commitment to the topic, or lack thereof. The most important aspect of f2f communication is accountability. Leaders should prefer communication this way because it facilitates "face-to-nametape" recognition. I can look into the person's eyes to ensure they have taken positive control of the information I am passing. By doing this in person, you'll know almost immediately if the person understands or not. Now you know exactly who will be carrying out whatever it is that you have communicated.

Communicating f2f also allows for questions, further explanation, etc. that other mediums don't allow. Leaders should never selectively add a buffer (text, email or phone call) if they don't have to. The recipient of the communication is less likely to ignore and shelve what you are communicating if you conduct it f2f. You can display your intent, which will, in turn, facilitate ownership by the recipient because the topic will likely facilitate a conversation versus a directive you send electronically. The secondary form of communication is via phone. If you are unable to physically conduct communication, then do it by phone. When you communicate using the phone, you can at least ensure the information has been received. By answering the phone, the recipient is telling you that they are listening (which may not always be true, but it's better than email). You are still able to elaborate, engage in a dialogue and display intent. The recipient is still able to gain ownership of the topic and the provider of the information is still able to keep the recipient accountable because the conversation occurred directly.

The third form of communication, and by far the worst form of communicating, is email. Unfortunately, email has become the primary mode of communication in most industries because it's easy. It's easy because it's fast. Leaders should remember, like everything else in the world, anything that is good or valuable takes time. When you use email, you lose the face-to-nametape recognition, accountability, true understanding and ownership. How many times in a meeting have you heard about how an email was sent describing an issue or task, just to hear that it wasn't received? Both the issuer and the recipient can hide behind their computers. "I sent an email two weeks ago that said this needed to be done and no one did it." "That's weird, I never received that email and I definitely would have completed it if I got it." The truth is the person or group almost certainly received the email. However, they likely receive anywhere from fifty to five hundred emails a day. If you think leaders are meticulously combing every email, then you're lying to yourself—especially if their role requires physical performance. It is infinitely more important that their computer is shut and that they are leading by example, motivating and influencing their people for 90% of their day. Some would likely counter with how email is now capable of receipt acknowledgments, and they should ensure the email is received. If that's your response, then you are truly the problem. Simply put, you cannot effectively communicate or lead via email. It's much more difficult to display intent as well as ensure the person understands what you're communicating and whether they have received or read it. If you are sending emails with important information and breathing a sigh of relief when pressing send, you are shirking responsibility. When there are crickets heard in the meeting about how no one has complied with an annual survey and the staff members say "I sent the email," they don't care about the team's success or it just isn't a priority.

Whenever you *have* to send an email because a physical conversation or phone call isn't possible, you must follow up. When an email is the only option, your next step should be to call the person and then try to physically find the person, essentially conducting the forms of communication in reverse. As a staff leader within the 75th Ranger Regiment, I was self-aware enough to understand and acknowledge that the majority of the people I would send emails to would never read them. So, after I would press send, I would walk to the office of the leader or person I needed a decision or action from. I would knock on the door if it was closed and only poke my head in to let them know what I had just sent, why I thought it was important and what I required to progress. That would usually initiate a discussion giving me the answer or information I needed—or at a minimum move my email up in priority, and I would always receive a response. Later on, I will provide some specific recommendations for email etiquette and correspondence rules. However, now that we have covered the three forms of communication, let's go over how to communicate.

A leader's communication should be clear, concise, and candid. The person receiving the information should not doubt what you were trying to convey. Think about how you would communicate a topic to a person with absolutely no experience in the topic you're discussing. That's the level of clarity, simplicity, and brevity you should be communicating in. It's not to offend anyone and or speak down to anyone, it's to ensure a complete understanding that results in a level of individual and collective ownership. The leaders and teams that do this the best perform like a machine. They fundamentally understand their roles, they are efficient, and they deliver results. When a leader communicates effectively in multiple instances, their staff, peers, and superiors will see the pattern. Because the team understands the pattern, they will operate more independently and exercise disciplined initiative. A leader will know if they communicated effectively if they have to "pull the reigns" a bit. They should admit to communicating poorly if they are consistently having to "kick people in the ass to move."

People remember the first thing that is said and the last thing that is said. That's it. Your most important points should be at the very beginning and the very end of any engagement. We see examples of this everywhere. How were you taught to write effectively? An introduction should contain a hypothesis—what it is you are trying to prove or disprove? It should be a problem statement that should immediately tell the reader what the piece is about and what your judgment is. The body should contain the criteria used to prove and disprove, implications of what you're providing and the detail required to inform the reader. The closing should summarize and re-emphasize your hypothesis, list the bottom-line evidence that proves or disproves it and provides the next required action. We also see this in the news. The first thing you see and hear is the breaking news headline. It's designed to draw you in. That headline is then discussed in a way that an attention span can support—who, what, when, where and why. Notice what news broadcasts do at the end of a show. They know that the majority of the content they just provided was dark, gloomy and mostly overwhelming negative, so what do they do? They tell a good news story. A soldier surprising their family with a no-notice homecoming, a dog that saved someone's life, etc. They thank you for your time before the program ends in an attempt to get you to return tomorrow. The news happens in this order because people remember the first thing seen or said, and they remember the last thing seen or said.

If you are unable to state your point or define your problem in two to three sentences, you don't understand the problem. Therefore, how can you expect others to understand? State your case upfront, describe, discuss and conclude. Let the recipient(s) of the information ask questions. Enter into a dialogue. If someone asks you a question, it's likely that others have the same question. Field them and use it as a teaching point for you and them. You learn more about something when you teach it because the perspective of others will educate you. So, anticipate questions before you communicate intent.

Candid communication means being sincere, truthful and straightforward. It' doesn't mean a leader should be quick to tell someone how awful they are at their job. Being candid is commonly mistaken for being mean or unnecessarily frank. Leaders should cultivate honest, unbiased feedback with the goal of building a culture of sincerity. They should be provided sincere feedback and be open to candid feedback as well. Most people take pride in being able to "speak truth to power" or "tell it like it is," but leadership candor is much more than this. Leaders should provide candid feedback consistently, to everyone. Leaders who only provide candid feedback to certain people breed dissent and potential favoritism. The quickest way to lose control as a leader is to hold your people to different standards. If you know an individual on your team doesn't respond well to sincere, candid feedback then it's your responsibility to change that. People often believe that it's extremely difficult to receive candid feedback. However, I would argue that it's much harder to give candid feedback than it is to receive it. It's hard because you have likely developed a relationship with the person you're providing feedback to and it's hard for us to transition and or separate personal relationships and our professional relationships. Ideally, everyone in the workplace understands that performance in business should be separated from personal relationships. However, people are human and so this concept needs to be introduced, educated and enforced to establish an open, resilient and healthy team. This is why some leaders usually advise their subordinate leaders not to develop friendships with their subordinates because people are generally unable to separate the two without causing discontent.

My recommendation to leaders on how to establish a culture of candor is to conduct leader development scenarios, learning development games or fun events that allow people to see the best and worst of each other. When you expose yourself to playful embarrassment, it shows that you're human and your subordinates will realize they don't have to be perfect to be a high performer. This is why organizations like professional sports teams and the military grow so close. They spend so much time together, conducting both physical and mental work, that it's inevitable that their weaknesses be exposed, resulting in a unity that most business atmospheres can't provide. After I left the Ranger Regiment and upon taking a leadership position in the business world, I immediately noticed that candid communication was an issue with my team. I knew that before we could change the culture of no candor on the collective team, I would first have to do it with the leaders, hoping it would become contagious from there. So, after the business week was complete and we were compiling the necessary reports before departing, I would write each of our names on a whiteboard with one arrow facing up and one arrow facing down. Then I would ask each leader, to include myself, to name one thing they did well (up arrow) and one thing they did poorly (down arrow) this week. We would first talk about own arrows and then we would give each other feedback on each other's performance. This immediately brought the leadership team closer together. Some people were surprised by what they heard about themselves and some people disagreed with comments made and required a more in-depth conversation. It was the healthiest exercise in candid communication we conducted, and it helped in bringing the team together.

Up to this point, we've talked about all of the things that should be communicated, how to communicate it and why. But we haven't discussed what shouldn't be communicated. Much like the risk of "thinking out loud," it's important that leaders maintain a positive mental attitude, foster a positive work environment and represent their organization as best they can. There is an excellent TED talk by Julian Treasure, a sound and communication expert called *How to Speak so That People Want to Listen* that I recommend that every leader listen to multiple times. I think he hits the nail on the head when he presents the "seven sins of speaking"—gossip, judging, negativity, complaining, excuses, lying and dogmatism. Ask yourself honestly, how often do you exercise one of the seven sins a day? Now ask yourself, who is present when you do? How often do you hear your subordinates or your employees exercise the seven sins in a day? If we are honest with ourselves, then it's fair to say that we probably lose our bearing in this regard multiple times a day. Think about how harmful this is for the team and your leaders. A leader who falls into the trap of voicing these sins in front of their subordinates or employees is breeding a negative work environment.

I understand that it's difficult to maintain a positive mental attitude when so many people around you may be negative, but it's your duty. Take ownership of the climate and culture of the organization by positively communicating. A mature and loyal leader will prevent others from speaking negatively about the company and its leaders. At a minimum, they will remove themselves from these scenarios when they occur. Notwithstanding, it's very natural to communicate frustrations, but we should do so in the proper settings. First, do so with a confidant. Someone that knows you are just trying to express frustration out loud. This is why our spouses usually know more about our work environment and its people than most people are willing to admit. If you need to do this at work, find a like-minded peer or even a superior and allow them to understand your intent. Disclose to them that you just need a moment to get something off your chest, or ask them if they can be a sounding board for a moment. Remember, if "Joe is always watching," then assume that "Joe is always listening" as well. Maintain high spirits, develop the culture of communication that you want to see. Make your organization a place where people want to work. Some days this will be tough, and sometimes even false motivation works. Trick your mind and body into improving your mood or day by smiling with your eyes, not just your mouth. Think about how good you have it. Keep things in perspective. Lastly, regardless of your position or industry, I would highly recommend that your opinions on politics, sexual orientation, and religion be left in the car. If these three topics are enough to divide families and be the root cause of warfare resulting in the death of countless people— you're an idiot if you think it won't cause an issue at work.

Effective communication is a two-way street. If you are the re- cipient of communication by a leader or you require guidance to be communicated, then you have responsibilities too—such as being easy to talk to. Give the leader or person communicating with you your attention. Ask questions if you need the leader to expound upon their point. If there is something you know is missing from the guidance given, ask specifically for it. The leader communicating with you will appreciate your interest and clarification. Imagine you have been with a company for significantly longer than the leader communicating to you and the team. This provides you a unique perspective that new leaders just haven't experienced yet. Arm them with your knowledge to ensure the team is successful. Communicate issues or friction points that you have experienced in your time there. A leader worth their weight will genuinely appreciate your feedback. This bottom-up feedback will allow the leader to communicate more clearly and with more detail to ensure an understanding. This is especially important when the organization you work for operates using a specific industry language, jargon, abbreviations, and acronyms. When this doesn't happen, it results in miscommunication. Miscommunication can have lasting effects on an individual's reputation and credibility and a team's overall performance and morale. Leaders who communicate well foster an environment of inclusion and honesty. They understand the power of language and use it to their advantage. They understand how to change or scale their communicative approaches to ensure their message resonates. Based on the feedback leaders receive, they learn who the informal leaders are and how influential informal leaders can be to the collective performance.

The last recommendation I will make regarding communication is to praise in public and punish in private. Highlight your team's individual and collective success so they understand why they train and work so hard. You will find that people will covet the opportunity to be recognized and will work harder, and more importantly, it is extremely fulfilling to congratulate or reward a subordinate in front of their peers and or family. Punish in private means do not make it a point to openly highlight a person's failure or issue. There is never any reason to purposely embarrass people. If you take the person aside, tell them what was expected of them and show them how they failed or executed a lapse in judgment, etc. The disappointment and embarrassment in themselves will likely be bad enough. Once you're finished delivering whatever information, correction or punishment the actions require, turn the correction into counseling. Build them back up and arm them with what they need to be successful.

PART I SUMMARY

Practice the above attributes and see how you, and those whom you lead, respond. These foundational principles will allow you to progress as a leader regardless of the position you hold. Remember that as a leader, you are expected to know when to lead, but it is equally important to know when to follow. Even leaders need to be led. Actively pursue mentors to guide you. Your mentor doesn't need to be someone older or in a higher position. They can be peers. Anyone who you can confide in, who listens and provides counsel. My final note on individual leadership, self-development, and growth is do more than what is asked of you, be accountable to yourself first and then to those around you, and acknowledge that you are responsible for everything that your team succeeds and fails to do.

PART II

LEADERSHIP BY POSITION: STAFF VS OPERATIONS

L eaders become well rounded by serving in multiple diverse
positions. As discussed in Part I, the foundational layer of leadership should not change based on your position. However,
it's perfectly acceptable that your leadership approach(s) change
based on the role that you fill. Regardless of industry, most people
and leaders can relate to the differences between being an operator
and being a staffer. Understanding the role and importance of both is
paramount in leading any group of people. True leaders understand
the value and purpose of both the staff and the organization's operators. Leaders who don't understand the value of both of these critical
components drive a wedge between the two proponents, and it results

in poor organizational performance and individualism. It is a leader's responsibility to create a shared understanding between these two elements to be successful. My intent for Part II is to define and describe the purpose of these two components as well as the responsibilities of the leaders within.

KNOW YOUR ROLE!

By the term "operator" I mean the operations officer or manager responsible for achieving the main objective or purpose of the organization. An operator on a sports team is the actual athlete. An operator in the military is the person conducting the physical mission. An operator in business ranges from the salesperson in the field to the operational manager on the floor of a distribution center or plant. By the term "staffer" I mean a member of the support team that facilitates the success of the operation. Staffers on a sports team are the physical trainers, scouts, and team administrators. Staffers in the military exist in sections from personnel, intelligence, logistics, communication, etc. Staffers in business exist in similar departments such as human resources, safety, IT, accounting, etc.

Leaders in charge of influencing both the operator and staff proponents should be quick to provide initial guidance in order to create a shared understanding of how you envision each proponent conducting business. A leader should provide this guidance and counsel down to the individual leader within each proponent and then bring all leaders together to share their vision and intent with the collective team. When this is done correctly, individual leaders, as well as the collective leadership team, know what is expected of them. Once a foundational understanding is established, the team can begin to progress forward, together. The benefits of providing both individual and collective guidance and intent to these proponents are that it will mitigate subordinate leaders or proponent representatives from prioritizing their own initiatives. There is nothing worse than watching operational managers and staff leaders attempting to prioritize their individual projects or goals based on their perceived self-importance. This happens when leaders and members of either proponent don't understand their purpose in the team's success.

When providing purpose to these proponents, I have found it beneficial to speak in scale, from large-to-small. In the business world, this means describing purpose at the industry level, company level, specific team level and finally the individual level. In the military, this means describing purpose from the strategic level, the operational level, the tactical level, and finally the individual level. Presenting purpose in this way will help your subordinates understand the effects of their decisions, both below them and above them. This will also prevent your proponent leaders from tunnel vision. Tunnel vision occurs when proponent leaders are only able to see the effects of decisions from their individual level and perspective.

For example, an operations leader presses send on an email on the 24th of December regarding his disappointment in the team's poor performance for the day and then provides corrective measures to improve. The leader who sent the email thought the message was appropriate and necessary, even though it's the day before Christmas. When staff leaders receive this email, it affects all of them differently.

The personnel or HR section quickly reverts to the fact that only a small percentage of people were present at work that day because of the holiday season, which explains the decrease in performance. The safety section perspective was that the day was more of a success than usual days because not a single person was injured throughout the day. The same can be said when operational leaders receive notes, calls or emails regarding perceived non-compliance in certain staff projects or initiatives.

Now, let's imagine that a staff leader provided an email on the 24th of December indicating that the operations team failed to produce "X" report or metric. The operations leader is astounded that this staff proponent dares to send an email of that type on the 24th of December. The operational leaders tell themselves that the staff leader has no idea what is important to the company and what challenges the operator faced that day, and they think about how this recurring report or metric is close to meaningless in completing the purpose or mission of the organization. We have all seen these scenarios and in fact, we probably observe them or facilitate them almost daily. This happens when leaders fail to communicate clear purpose, guidance, and prioritization to their organization's operators and staff.

IMPLIED AND SPECIFIED TASKS

It's important for leaders, in either proponent to understand and internalize their purpose. They should do this by understanding what is implied and what is specified. *Implied tasks* are implicit actions that leaders should inherently do based on their role and position as a leader. A *specified task* is one that is essential to mission success and is explicitly stated to ensure understanding. With those definitions in mind, what is the purpose of a staff? Whenever I ask staff leaders this question, they say "to advise the boss on everything concerning X"—"X" can represent human resources, intelligence, accounting, safety, etc. This answer isn't wrong per se, but it is weak and it lacks awareness. Of course, your purpose is to advise the boss on whatever your specialty is! That's why you were hired, it is your #1 *implied* task. The more complete, leader-driven and self-aware answer is "to alleviate stress on subordinate or operational elements in order to facilitate mission success for the organization." This answer applies to any organization that has a staff. A staff's #1 *specified* task is to assist and support the operational team in their mission. A staff leader should contain the individual awareness, perspective, and humility to understand that operators are the customers of the staff. Great leaders serving in staff roles understand that they are the *supporter*, not the *supported*. They understand that support structures exist to improve the operation.

THE SUPPORTER AND THE SUPPORTED

With that realization in mind, it's worth covering the purpose of an operational leader and addressing how often they may misuse or abuse the staff because of their misunderstanding of their role and the role of the staff. An operational leader is charged with influencing the people responsible for completing the purpose of the organization. For example, if the company's purpose is to receive and ship boxes based on customer orders, then the employees of the operational leader are the ones moving the boxes. The employees moving the boxes from point A to point B are the customers of the operational leader. The operational leader is the *supporter* of those employees and is *supported* by the staff. Operational leaders who misunderstand their role in the organization believe they are to be *supported* by everyone. They wrongly believe that the staff literally works for them and therefore, they abuse the staff to meet their individual goals. An operational leader's #1 implied task is to manage the people in their completion of whatever makes the company money. An operational leader's #1 *specified* task is to work collaboratively with the support staff to maximize the organization›s proficiency in its mission to deliver results. The best operational leaders understand and openly acknowledge the hard and sometimes thankless work of the staff. They look for staff support expertise and operational staff recommendations to build a cohesive team, which will in turn yield operational results.

I have observed multiple organizations struggle with managing the personalities associated with the staff versus operations topic. There are a couple of simple truths that ought to be acknowledged when discussing this dynamic for context. First, the leader of the company is likely an operator. Second, any organization that values leadership requires its leaders to serve in both operational and staff positions. This experience allows leaders to personally and professionally develop while maintaining a humble perspective. Third, true leaders usually openly admit that the difference between a good organization and a great organization is the staff. Think about professional sports, for example. If all professional athletes in one sport contain generally the same amount of talent, as in they are good enough to play at the professional level, then what is it that makes them champions? It's the dedication, servanthood, and competency of the team's staff. The coaching *staff* designs plays to cultivate and enable individual and collective talent. It's the trainers that identify player strength and weakness. It's the team's medical staff that makes the players sustainable and resilient over a season. It's the player's agents, team administrators and logisticians that ensure the players are financially secure so they can focus on their operational performance.

In Fortune 500 businesses, what is the difference between two organizations in the same industry? It's the competency of their staff that facilitates operational performance. It's a business's legal advisor that keeps the business from any unforeseen or catastrophic legal issues. It's the human resources staff that actively conducts talent acquisition and talent retention to ensure operational superiority. It's the software engineer that designs a stellar product for the salesperson to deliver with confidence. In the special operations community, it's the logistics element that ensures our nation's most competent operators are enabled with world-class equipment to match their individual skill. It's the intelligence staff that arms the operators with a level of detail and refinement that facilitates mission success and the safe return of all operators.

WHY BOTH ARE CRITICAL

The leader of an organization with operators and a staff is required to support both proponents equally. They are responsible for conducting the expectation management required to ensure both elements understand their roles. Leaders who cultivate the competence of both their operators and their staff will have a level of cohesion that makes the operational process look easy. Ideally, both proponents make service and support of each other an implied task. When this happens, the team can navigate extremely difficult tasks together and a leader is better prepared to challenge their organization with complex, specified tasks to drive real, tangible innovation.

PART III

INDIVIDUAL AND COLLECTIVE LEADERSHIP BUSINESS

PROFESSIONAL LEADERS

Leadership is a profession that stands alone. It should not matter whether or not you are a staff leader or an operations leader. Part of the inherent responsibility and honor of being a leader is that you are expected to be a steward to the profession. A profession requires expertise and trust. Now, measure your industry and your leadership position with those two criteria. Can you say with confidence that you are a professional? Not *are* you professional, but are you *a* professional? Does the general public recognize your position as a profession? Expertise implies training, education, and experience. Trust is a belief or confidence in the ability of a person or position. For example, we can probably agree that being a physician is a profession. Their position requires extensive training, clinical study and research. Additionally, because of a physician's training and education, the public generally provides physicians with a large amount of trust. With expertise and trust as our criteria for a profession, I am sure most Americans would argue that being a politician is not a profession. Politicians are usually educated and intellectual folks, however, they are likely the least trusted people in the nation. Professionals dominate the details of their craft and being a leader is no different. Regardless of your industry, there are some basic leadership functions a leader should perform to be effective. There are some common denominators that all leaders should exercise when coming into a new position, maintaining readiness and conducting daily business. The following will provide some recommendations on how to lead any group of people.

When taking on a new leadership position, it's important to give yourself and the team you are inheriting time to assess. Assessment periods vary based on multiple factors but include the number of people you lead. The more people you lead, the longer it will take to assess individual and team performance. If you are chosen to be a leader in an industry or company that requires immediate and consistent, quantifiable results or in a company that maintains a high operational tempo, then your assessment time will likely be condensed. Regardless of your position or industry, a leader should always take time to assess. Your first interaction with the team shouldn't be an introduction quickly followed by a list of changes that are coming.

People who do this openly undermine the effort and actions of the team and leaders they replace. Respect the experience of the team, the relationships developed by the previous leader and the fact that you are an outsider. A newly appointed leader's responsibility is to listen, observe and assess.

Keep in mind that your team will likely know more about you than you think. They will naturally assume that change is coming, and they are hoping that you will not be the type of leader who makes snap assessments, judgments, and drastic changes. When you are made aware that you will assume a new leadership position, take the time to write down 1) What you know 2) What you think you know 3) What you don't know and you would like to know. It's impossible to know what you don't know, but at least you will have a starting point to build from. Another list to start compiling is what your goals and priorities will be for the assessment period. Good leaders will have done some research into the position, the team, their performance and will, therefore, be able to make some logical assumptions for improvement. However, your notes are for you and shouldn't be openly vocalized just yet. A good senior leader will give you some guidance, direction, and purpose to help start your assessment process. Additionally, because people will know that you have been selected for this leadership position, some will make the attempt to sway your thought process, gain your support and set conditions for their individual success. You'll receive this in a couple of different ways. People will come to you with gossip, they'll start adding you onto email chains that they never have before, and some will candidly come to you with things you should change right way once you take the leadership position. You should hear these people out, and make mental note of the topics, but don't let them inject bias into your assessment! Leaders who do this don't realize that they are picking sides before they even understand what side is what.

Make an honest attempt to walk into the door with zero assumptions or preconceived notions. Allow the collective team and its individual members to be observed by you with *a tabula rasa,* a blank slate. Everyone should start with an "A" until proven otherwise; give the team the benefit of the doubt. Be approachable, ask questions and meet as many people as possible. Any decent organization will have an onboarding process that facilitates your in-processing and assessment. If they don't, make it yourself. Focus first on the administrative permissions and authorities your position requires to operate. This will allow you to meet the staff and build lasting relationships. Next, understand the battle rhythm of leadership events. You should be provided a list of recurring daily, weekly and monthly occurrences that require leadership presence and/or action. This should provide you with a macro-level understanding of your daily flow, which in turn provides you with what is most important—spending time with your people as they complete the purpose of the organization. Most importantly, spend time with the people you are charged to lead, at the lowest possible level. During your assessment period, the organization has yet to recognize you as the person to go to for everything concerning that team, but soon they will. So, take advantage of that assessment period to be with the people who do the hardest work. Display your work ethic, ask them questions and just listen to their perspective. They are who you work for.

After your assessment you should have an understanding of who and where you can go to for help and support; a general understanding of each major function of your team; an understanding of the climate or culture (depending on how long your assessment period has been) of the team and an understanding of what the team needs from your leadership to be successful. You should have also gained an understanding of whatever specific function or aspect your leader has specified to you, such as property accountability, inventory, specific subordinates, and the support staff. Your assessment should be deliberately compiled as a document of reference, which will help keep you honest about your priorities and the development of your team. You should share and/or brief this document and its findings to the people "above" you and "below" you. You owe the person paying you what your leadership assessment is and how you plan to progress. Your senior leaders will let you know what they think, provide refined guidance and ask questions. Your subordinate leaders or team need to hear your assessment! It will justify what you intend to change or improve. They will appreciate your perspective and be introduced to your thought process, goals and initiatives. When good leaders do this right, they gain credibility. You should provide this feedback at the individual and collective level through counseling and communication. Providing feedback this way will prevent your intent from being diluted as it makes its way from you to the lowest possible level.

Now that your assessment period has concluded and you have communicated your findings, it's time to deliver your intent and priorities. Your intent should be clear, directly tied to your organization's mission or purpose and have a suspense, i.e., tied to time. Establishing priorities is critical when leading any team or organization. You have to make clear what is actually important. The company or organization that doesn't have real and true priorities will receive compliance from their leaders, but not commitment. How many times have you been told by a boss that an issue at the forefront is a priority? I have seen this often—especially in large, results-driven organizations. The larger an organization is, the less likely it is that everyone understands its priorities. Further, the larger an organization is, the more likely it is that priorities change and differ because of the niche and specific sections that the organization has. Which equates to more priorities. In many organizations, there are more "priorities" than there are hours in a day. So, make your priorities realistic and meaningful. The bottom line is, if everything is a priority, then nothing is a priority. The purpose of establishing real priorities is to communicate to subordinates what they should be spending their time on and where you, as their leader, are willing to assume risk. Real priorities are enduring and specific. They are enduring because they are difficult to complete, require commitment and involve organizational success. Have you ever been in an organization that didn't know how to prioritize? This could be because it focused on prioritizing everything, or nothing at all, or provided such a vague priority that it can be interpreted in too many ways. This is a real problem that causes subordinate leaders and members of a team to lose faith in their leaders because they fail to understand what is important. When priorities are not established and enforced, people apply their effort to what they chose, which may not be in the best interest of the greater organization. They wrongly assume risk on your behalf and make the team less effective.

INDIVIDUAL LEADERSHIP BUSINESS

Individual leader readiness is required to set an example for those to follow and will ultimately inform your superiors that you're ready for the next level. Individual leaders should be good at the following:

Take notes: Always have something to write on and write with. If you're the leader who has to borrow these items or is always writing on a piece of ripped computer paper, then you're sending the message that you're unprepared. When a leader is speaking, take notes. It shows you're paying attention, that you're interested and that you value their time and perspective.

Know your audience: You should be able to communicate with an individual or a group in their own terms in order to influence their thinking. How would you communicate a lack of performance to a senior HR member vs a senior operations member? How would you describe a process change to a superior vs a subordinate?

Know your boss: How does your boss or leader receive information? Written form, via slides, a whiteboard or just a conversation over lunch? It's your job to figure that out. Don't be a generational snowflake that thinks a senior leader's entire purpose is to figure out how you tick, because it's actually the exact opposite.

Know your boss's priorities: If it's important to them, it's now important to you. Your priorities should be a refined version of your boss's priorities, and don't overthink it. Have your priorities, your immediate bosses' priorities and his boss's priorities written down and easily accessible. When people see you referring to them, they will be impressed with your ability to understand intent two levels above yourself. When your subordinates see you do this, they'll realize they should be doing it too and they will help disseminate your priorities to the lowest possible level. Priorities are a leader's way of telling a subordinate what to spend their time on.

Speak your boss's language: Every time your boss or leader speaks or communicates, you should be learning. Communicate with them in the way they communicate with you. If you pay close enough attention or spend enough time with your boss or leader, you will notice patterns of communication and specific language. When you use that language back to them, they can immediately relate and they appreciate your attention to detail. This will allow you to influence them to support you, your team or your initiatives.

Always have questions ready: You never know when an opportunity for development will present itself. Whether it's your boss grabbing you to go to lunch with a senior executive on five minutes' notice or when you're at your kid's sporting event and a boss of yours has a kid on the opposite team, etc. We rarely think of meaningful questions on the fly, so save yourself the embarrassment and think of them and write them down in the notebook that you should always be carrying.

How to deliver bad news to your boss: If your leader knows you, they will know right away that you have bad news to deliver. Deliver it! No one cares about the meaningless fluff people decorate problems with. It will make the recipient angrier when you pussyfoot around the problem. 1) Provide a bottom-line up front (BLUF). 2) Provide the 5W's—who, what, when, where and why as completely, yet concisely as possible. 3) Provide a recommended solution to the problem. Give your leader a menu of options to choose from. Never surprise your leader or put them in a position to make a snap decision when they aren't required to do so at that moment.

Be ready to pitch an elevator brief: If you think you're busy, think about how busy your leaders are. Sometimes your leader will see you in the hall in passing, they'll signal you or tell you to walk with them. They'll tell you they are on their way to an important meeting on a subject you can advise them on. They'll ask you for the two-minute synopsis on a very difficult topic while they wait for the elevator or while standing outside of the room the meeting is occurring in. Remember, the first thing and the last thing you say will be what they retain. Provide the BLUF, two to three points for discussion and most importantly, the "So what." Tell them why it's important.

You will have enemies: Come to terms with the fact that some people just won't want you to be successful. They do this out of their own insecurities and jealousy. Don't sweat the small the stuff; focus on the good in people and let these people watch you progress. If you're doing your job right, you'll acquire enemies. It's impossible to please everyone. Your job is to advocate for the people that work for you. Real team players will understand this and will hopefully get over it, some won't. Too bad.

Fire and forget: Results based organizations are exactly that. Don't be offended or take it personally when you are corrected or even yelled at. There may be reasons that you can't control that led to that event, so give your leaders the benefit of the doubt. Take the verbal lashing, pick your head up and keep moving.

Make a decision: Stop blaming a "lack of guidance" for your inability to make a decision out of fear of being wrong or failing. You were chosen to lead for a reason. Do it. It's better to ask for forgiveness than for permission. If it's not illegal, immoral or unethical, use your best judgment with the information you have to execute your plan violently or not at all.

LEADER CORRESPONDENCE RULES

1   The *To* line is for decision and action. Recipients on the To line are required to comply, commit, act or decide and most importantly, respond. If a subordinate sends you an email, you owe them feedback. The *Carbon Copy* (CC) line is for awareness. Recipients on the CC line are not required to respond, but require awareness of the information. Never *blind carbon copy* (BCC) someone on an email. It's a coward move. It will only cause confusion and issues.

2   The *Subject* line is important. It determines if it'll be read or not. If you can convey your issue, question or topic in the subject, it's that much easier for the recipient to see and respond. However, if all your emails contain "Hot email," "Highly important" and other forms of flare, it will take away credibility from legitimately important emails. You can even create a standard for this to help people weed through what is important and what isn't. For example, "For Awareness" in the subject line means you want people to be advised on the subject, but no decision is required. "For Decision" lets the recipient know that the subject requires a response from a decision-maker and that the process or issue will hold in place until the decision is made and distributed. "For Action" means the message requires action and progress with

commitment and compliance. If this option is used effectively, it will contain a "why" portion, making its execution incredibly efficient.

3 Never send an emotional email. You'll regret it. If possible, have someone else read your email or your response and see how they interpret it. Take a walk before pressing send. Don't *Reply All* unless you need to. Crushing people's emails with a topic they don't care about will only cause animosity and the thread will get unprofessional, pretty quickly. Never forward an email without reading the thread. Lazy leaders do this and call it "delegation." It's not. Read the thread, interpret and filter the information and summarize it for the reader in your own words. Sometimes you'll find out that the forward isn't necessary.

4 If I need to scroll down multiple times to continue reading your email/fiction novel, consider it not read and deleted. Emails should contain a BLUF, bullets or discussion points and then a "So What" to tell me why it's important. Leaders will let you know if they want or need more information. With that said, I acknowledge that there are times when this is unavoidable. That's fair enough—just don't make it a habit or your name will be associated with the rule "forward to junk."

5 Make an *out-of-office* message if you are going to be out of work for more than 24 hrs. The auto-reply message should be a point of contact for the person covering for you at work and a way to reach you in case of an emergency. You still have a customer service and leadership responsibility to help people at work even though you're not present. Don't gloat about where you

are or what you are doing while everyone else is working. First, no one cares. Second, it's petty.

6 Don't be the leader with a full inbox, unable to receive or send emails. It's an indicator of laziness and it's no one else's responsibility but your own. In most cases nowadays, a computer and email are our weapons systems. Maintain it.

7 Respond! Responding is the next best thing to being present. You show your team that you are present by providing feedback, encouragement, and correction if required. There is nothing more discouraging than receiving guidance to complete something, providing proof and support to that guidance and never receiving any feedback or a response to your efforts. You're basically saying, "I don't care about you or what you're telling me."

STAFF FUNDAMENTALS

Your purpose (why you exist) is to alleviate stress on subordinate elements for them to complete the mission or goal of the organization. You are the supporter, not the supported. This is implied to great leaders, but needs to be explicitly explained to average leaders.

Your mission (what you do) is to simplify and advise. You should never expect a leader of a large, high performing organization to be a subject matter expert in your area. They simply have way more to do and to lead than you do. Simplify complex problems for the leader above you and advise them on your findings and recommendations. This should be implied to all staff leaders.

Based on your position and proximity to senior leaders, you will likely spend more time with the boss or leader than their operational leaders. Use this access to better the organization by keeping other staff leaders and operational leaders informed of what you know and hear. You owe them warning, information, and support as you should genuinely want your peers and operators to be successful. This is how you earn trust. Don't confuse this with an opportunity to spread rumors or gossip.

As a staff leader, you can significantly contribute to the organization's success by communicating and disseminating your leaders' intent, plans, and considerations. If you have been on a staff for a while, you have probably watched an operations leader or another staff leader briefing the boss on a topic that you know the boss or leader isn't going to support or approve. It's painful to watch, and it's partly your fault because you have been in the room with this leader enough times to know exactly how they feel about the issue and you should have contacted this leader and set conditions for their success. Because you are so observant, you probably even know the language this leader uses when the topic is addressed. As a staff leader in the 75th Ranger Regiment, I would make it a point to contact the company commanders (operational leaders) after every meeting that I felt would affect their companies plans, future briefs or schedules. I did this to ensure they weren't surprised by the boss's response and could make the necessary adjustments to their internal plans. At the very minimum, I could tell them what mood the boss was in, which would help them decide how their information should be delivered. Senior leaders expect this from their staff members. When this doesn't happen, it results in embarrassing moments of correction for the operational leaders, time wasted re-iterating the same topics repeatedly (depending on the size of your organization), and an unspoken level of disappointment in the staff for not informing and distributing information to operational leaders. Leaders who do this correctly build lasting personal relationships, make the organization more efficient and more cohesive.

Make *Standalone* products. That means, regardless of the form of communication used (f2f, text, email, memo, PowerPoint or phone) you should communicate in a way that allows the information you are providing to be understood by as many people as possible. If you're communicating something via PowerPoint slides, a memo or executive summary, your product should be able to provide the information in totality, without you saying anything at all. Products that stand alone assume the recipient knows nothing at all about the topic at hand. Your leaders will tell you to brief or communicate by exception if they choose, but it's their choice.

Place yourself between the problem and the boss. Don't escalate issues that don't require the attention of a senior leader. You're in a leadership position to solve problems for the boss. So, if you're the kind of "leader" who just forwards problems and solutions from one side to another, you're a paperweight. Great staff leaders place themselves between friction points. Most of the time that means taking on the problems that are too hard for others to complete. Staff leaders that do this well stop people from going to a senior leader to complain about how hard their job is. Little do they know, if they were to make it into the leader's office, the leader would take ownership of the problem—and believe me when I tell you things would get worse from there. This just in: your senior leader was probably you at some point, and they likely know your role and its difficulties better than you do. So don't make them do their job *and* your job too.

See around corners. Anyone can react, but leaders proactively anticipate through proper planning. It's impossible to plan every single branch or sequel that may occur. If your plan involves people (which all of them do) something will happen that you didn't anticipate, but you should be flexible and adaptable enough not to panic when it does.

Be the Bridge and the Barrier. By the *Bridge*, I mean your job is to get to "yes." Actualize and resource your leader's intent. Unless your boss is asking something of you that is illegal, immoral, unethical or scientifically impossible—your answer is "yes." That doesn't only apply to your boss or leader. If an operational leader, aka your customer, proposes a change in your area or discipline, and that change improves their operational experience or alleviates stress from their process—your answer is "yes." Any innovative change that happens in a company is done through the staff. Don't be the leader that says no because it's hard. By the *Barrier*, I mean be the devil's advocate, so the boss doesn't have to. There will be times when your leader will be placed in positions to make a decision or pick a side that will negatively affect morale or an important relationship. Sometimes this happens when subordinate leaders team up to pitch a plan that they have become emotionally invested in—maybe too emotionally invested in. Your senior leader will know that stopping this plan will cause resentment, and that resentment will lead to a perceived lack of trust or support. Great staff leaders can spot this when it happens. They become an invisible barrier, placing themselves in a position to deescalate the situation, or worst-case scenario, take the brunt of the perceived lack of support so the senior leader can maintain the trust and loyalty of their operations leaders. This is a complete art in staffing.

Be a participant, not an observer. If you're looking for the quickest way to gain zero credibility; talk and don't walk. Staff leaders should be intimately familiar with what their operators go through. They should be familiar with all the senses of completing the organization's mission. You don't want to approve the funding to ensure all our members get the footwear necessary to sustain what we do? That's fine, I will see you at 0200 in the morning, we're going for a twenty-mile ruck march. I can't wait to see the blood squirt from your boots once you apply downward pressure on every down step, I bet you'll approve the funding then. "Hi HR leader, oh you want me to deliver the news that an employee had her vacation disapproved at the last possible minute because you just didn't get to it. Okay, come with me and you tell her because the vacation was to attend a family funeral. Let's see how you lead yourself through that."

There are few things more frustrating as a professional leader who volunteers for the hardest possible assignments than to watch a staff "leader" and supposed peer about to fall asleep watching an unrelated YouTube video. You approach their desk covered in sweat and dirt from completing the organization's mission and you notice a cookie on a folded napkin next to their computer while perfectly dressed and clean. Staff leaders and members should go out of their way to do the part of the job that sucks! It will provide you valuable perspective, humility, and awareness. Standing alongside an operator while they complete the work will show them you care, that you're interested, and that you're committed.

COLLECTIVE LEADERSHIP BUSINESS

Know the importance of process discipline and knowledge management. High performing organizations simply cannot survive without processes. Every organization, from the team to the industry level, can have standard operating procedures (SOP), but if they don't have the discipline to follow them, they're useless and really only there if an audit occurs. Standards ought to be realistic, as simple as possible, and updated. The standard shouldn't be a hindrance to actual execution. It should be a guide for how to complete a task. If the process to complete the task is more rigorous than the task itself, no one will do it. Part of a leader's legacy is process discipline because the processes put in place should last longer than the leader. Does the process you have in place still work? Do you have processes just because the organization has always had them or because "you've always done it that way?" When is the last time you accessed the process when operating? Does the newest member of your team know about the process or need it to complete their job? Lastly, don't let an outdated standard be a barrier to success. I would argue that the odds are pretty high that people were able to complete the task without a standard. The topic at hand was standardized for one of two reasons. First, someone didn't complete the task correctly and it caused some rare yet catastrophic injury or loss which resulted in providing a level of direction that is embarrassing to most. Second, the process itself has become so convoluted that step-by-step directions are required to complete it. Be the leader who establishes processes to make completion of a task easier. The individual user should be able to apply their commitment to that task, which results in proficiency and speed.

As a leader in a constantly evolving technological world, knowledge management is important. Make it easy for people to use technology or they simply won't use it. If the group isn't using it, it's because the process sucks. Fix it or go analog and most importantly, don't be afraid to go analog—it's how the world did business for generations. How many websites must you access to complete your job? Currently, I honestly have to simultaneously monitor fifteen separate sites to observe operational performance, safety compliance, and employee engagement. This is why leaders in our current age bury their faces in a computer and lead people through email. If it takes more than three button clicks to find known information, your knowledge management is probably a mess. The best way a leader manages knowledge at the individual level is with a permanent, well-structured notebook. If you're already wed to a notebook, try leaving it in the car for three hours and see how many things or people you forget to engage. The only way to conduct productive knowledge management is for you to learn what isn't important—and get rid of it. Next, see what and where the team uses the most and then prioritize those locations, sites or documents. Finally, employ analytical effort and leadership emphasis into their utilization, ease of access and improvement. Proper knowledge management provides a level of continuity that we can't rely on people to provide over time. People vary in their level of individual effort, competence, and commitment. A leader should use knowledge management and process discipline to benefit from *past* performance, guide *present* performance and prepare for *future* performance.

Don't be surprised by Christmas and learn from everything that you do—everything. Have you ever been part of an organization that allows itself to be surprised by things they shouldn't be, like a known event? For example, if you know that your organization usually conducts a Christmas party, you shouldn't be surprised by its annual arrival. In a more practical example, if you know your organization will participate in the same two to five major events each year, then we would deduce that every year, event performance should improve, right? Wrong. This happens for a couple of reasons. First, if you improperly plan or don't plan at all for the execution of the event by hiding behind the fact that "we do it every year," you will fail, or at a minimum, plateau. Second, people change. It's logical to assume that every year, these events are likely new to at least some of your people. This is why it's important to properly plan, execute the event with a beginner's mind and more important than the execution, compile lessons learned. Record them in a way to ensure those lessons are incorporated into future execution. Leaders who fail to do this prevent their team from being part of a learning organization.

The military's planning process and doctrine is extensive, elaborate and tedious. I would argue that sometimes it's so extensive that planning becomes the event instead of the tool used to prepare for the event. Depending on the event, sometimes you spend more time training to plan than you do in training for the task required. With that said, my experience in using the military decision-making process has been humbling and rewarding. I was, and still am, very impressed with its attention to detail and standardization. I, in no way, believe I could reiterate its detail and true value in this book. Nor do have I the audacity or hubris to opine on the regulatory doctrine of a leadership organization that has been successfully planning for the better part of two hundred and fifty years. There are, however, some basic planning considerations that are effective in any organization that leaders should employ to ensure success. They are the military's most basic leading and planning procedures known as the troop leading procedures (TLPs), and they can absolutely be converted to any organization or industry as a fundamental planning rubric. Below is a quick conversion from the actual TLP's to apply to regular civilian leaders.

Receive the task: Acknowledge ownership of the task or event with the issuing authority, likely a superior of yours. Ask questions while you can, paying attention to detail. Make sure that you walk away knowing as much as you can about the task you were given. At the very minimum, try to extrapolate the 5W's (who, what, when, where and why) of the task or event. The clock starts here.

Make the team aware: Let your people know what you know. They will be less likely to execute one of the seven sins of speech we discussed earlier if they have received a warning of what's coming. You can be sure they are going to find out one way or another. If you let the rumor mill inform them of what's coming, you'll have to spend more time than you would like weeding through the make-pretend, emotional assumptions that people add to what they originally heard. Your people will appreciate that their leader informed them of a task or issue that will affect them—especially when you need those very people to act upon the task. They will be the ones executing what you plan. So, the sooner and more inclusive you are with your people, the more likely they are to take ownership of *their* plan. Some leaders are hesitant to do this because they are scared by the number of questions they receive. True leaders embrace these questions and then make the questions theirs. True leaders will use those questions because they likely didn't ask them upon receipt of the task. Listening to the questions of your subject matter experts will inform you of what needs to be addressed in the final plan. Be honest with them, let them know that you have just recently received this task and more details will follow. They will appreciate your honesty.

Make a tentative plan: depending upon the complexity of the event or task, most good leaders start brainstorming courses of action to execute the task before they're even done receiving it. Be careful with this—it may facilitate a set of blinders that will give you tunnel vision to other perspectives because you'll convince yourself that you have a near-immediate solution and it will, therefore, cause you to consciously or sub-consciously turn away different courses of action. However, your immediate thought process or gut response shouldn't be neglected. These gut reactions allow you to address macro-level aspects of a plan with ideas that are likely the simplest, which is why you thought of them so quickly. Take some time after receiving the task to compile notes, whether it be on a whiteboard or in a notebook. If you know you'll be using the whiteboard to distribute your plan to the team at a later time, it's a good place to start because it'll reveal your thought process to the team. Break apart the task in phases, either by time or by the event. Compile a way for phase objectives and milestones to be tracked to ensure progression. You can later assign ownership by delegating these sub-tasks to members of your team.

Initiate movement by compiling stakeholders. Make initial contact with the people you think you'll need to execute this plan well. Build relationships with staff members, operators, and outside professionals by empowering them to be part of the team and to contribute. Develop a timeline and a frequency to meet with people, both individually and as a team. It's important to do both individual and collective sessions because you'll find people become more and more reclusive the larger the team becomes. Also, you want to be a good steward of their time and experience. Meeting with an individual after a collective group sometimes reveals an opinion that wasn't mentioned in the team meeting because they "didn't want to make waves" or "they didn't want to shoot down their idea in front of the team." Remember that for the most part, people are very non-confrontational and it's better to consume your own time with both individual and collective meetings than have the entire team regret going to your meeting and only contributing a small percentage of what they're capable of.

Observe and conduct reconnaissance. Again, depending upon the nature of the event or task, take the necessary time to observe the location of execution. That means conduct multiple site surveys and venue visits to observe the location of the event or task. If the venue for the event is an outside location, take someone else with you, as two sets of eyes/experiences are better than one. If the event or task is occurring where you normally conduct business, you should still observe and recon it! Remove any bias from your mind about the area or venue and attempt to see the location through the lens of someone else simply participating in the event. Mold your mind around the purpose of the event or task when you recon the venue. Approaching your observation with this mindset will add value, regardless of whether or not you are already familiar with the location.

Complete the plan. At this point, you fully own the task. You have already told your team the task, so they're not surprised and they have started individually planning. You have already made a tentative plan with the information you had, which should have provided you a list of things that you didn't know and needed to find out as you refine the plan. You've built a team to help you, constructed a timeline with milestones for action and understand the capabilities and expertise of the stakeholders. Most recently, you observed the venue or location in which the task will be executed. You approached it with the task at the forefront of your mind, brought a team member with you for another perspective and made copious notes to ensure the domination of detail. Remember that pictures and videos are much more useful than your notes. Pictures speak a thousand words. Now you have what you need to refine your plan and ensure it is as completely as possible. Remember, we have already talked about how a plan only lasts to the first contact, so don't get wrapped up in trying to plan for every possible contingency. Make a decision and plan to execute violently with the information you have. If time permits, provide a draft of the plan you intend to distribute to your superior or the person who issued you the task. Their endorsement, support, and concurrence are vital. The last thing you want to do is disseminate the plan and your boss sees it at the same time as everyone else and then they immediately contact you with corrections, questions, and concerns. Providing the plan to the issuer before its distributed or published should act as a conditions-check of how completely you and your team prepared. You will also learn about aspects of the task or event that may have changed that you were unaware of.

Distribute the plan. There is a difference between dissemination and distribution. Distribution is more deliberate, calculated and controlled. Dissemination is a shotgun blast intended for a less refined, all-encompassing audience. Think of it this way: Fortune 500 retail and logistics companies have distribution centers, not dissemination centers. When distributing the plan, I recommend utilizing the proper forms of communication and the method under *Prior* in the counseling and mentorship section. The probability of your people having questions is high, and in fact, you should encourage questions. Provide them with a soft or hard copy of the plan first, and let them digest it. This will make the meeting and discussion you have after distribution much more valuable. With that said, don't wait for conditions to be perfect. If the suspense to action is short notice, deliver it in person and adjust as necessary. Ensuring your subordinates have the necessary time to plan and adjust is infinitely more important than waiting until you think the timing is perfect. The timing will never be perfect!

When you find yourself worrying about the right time to distribute the plan, think about the 1/3—2/3 rule. The 1/3—2/3 rule states that leaders should spend no more than 1/3 of their time in the planning phase while the remaining 2/3's of time be given to your subordinates or team members. They will be the ones responsible for executing the required task, so give them the necessary time to understand and prepare their team to ensure successful completion. Don't be the leader who hordes information. People are people, and as they talk, rumors will spread and information will be taken out of context or manipulated as it is passed from person to person. For example, let's say after an annual culminating event or at the end of a fiscal year your organization usually makes some significant personnel and leadership changes. The longer you wait to effectively distribute the plan for moves and why the moves are occurring, the more disgruntled and unsupported your subordinates will feel. Aspects of this decision that leaders sometimes forget or neglect are the second and third-order effects of what they assume to be a relatively seamless change. Think about the potential life changes your subordinates may have to make to complete what you're asking of them. Aspects include child care, schooling, medical conditions, transportation, etc. This is in addition to the professional implications, such as talent management, working relationships, mentorship, development and career progression for the junior leaders under the leader you are moving. This is why the 1/3-2/3 rule is so important. For this scenario, the best way to distribute this information would be the following: Compile the information required to make a deliberate decision; deliver this information personally first; provide the *why* and be prepared to be precise, especially if you know your decision is going to be perceived as a negative change to the subordinate; and complete these steps with as many people as required given the amount of changes you have decided upon. Depending on the number of moves you planned to make, one or two of them aren't going to work based on multiple factors, such as family situation, leaving the organization, etc. Next, distribute the totality of leadership changes to all leaders en masse. This will ensure the proper message and intent are delivered and will prevent rumors about why changes are happening. It will also inform the changing leaders of their new counterparts and points of contact. Finally, encourage your newly formed teams to disseminate the information as necessary. If done correctly, all members of the team, including support staff, will understand the essentials associated with the change and the business can progress as required.

Manage, supervise and refine. Once the plan has been distributed, manage the necessary resources to support your subordinate leaders as they plan. Supervise their planning process and refine the plan based on what you observe to ensure success. Lead your subordinates through their planning process. Ensure they train and rehearse for execution. Training and rehearsals are critical to ensuring maximum performance, regardless of the task. Whether the task is an oral presentation, a telephone conference, a product or process launch, or a tactical operation, they all require training and rehearsals. Train to the hardest possible standard while enforcing safety to ensure planned contingencies are addressed and mitigated. Rehearse to ensure everyone knows their job and the job of those around them. As meaningless or minute as some details may seem, no detail cannot be dominated through rehearsals. Rehearsing the conference call, for example, may reveal that no one reserved a venue for the call to occur; it may reveal the number provided for the call was incorrect or changed; it may reveal that the audio feature on the phone was broken or non-functional; it may reveal that the recipient is unable to hear when you are in a certain part of the room, etc. The lesson here is, if I can rattle off five possible contingencies with a simple phone call, what does that tell us about how detailed our rehearsals need to be for a major project launch or an operation?

Compile lessons learned. This is where both the individual and the collective fail, simply because it's hard to stay disciplined after completion of the task. The amount of time invested to plan, train, rehearse and then execute is exhausting, depending on the task. Because of that fact, we tend to mentally, emotionally and physically divorce ourselves from the task as soon as it's complete, even when we know we'll have to execute that task again—whether it be tomorrow, next week, next quarter or next year. Leaders need to be disciplined enough to focus on the future, and part of that is learning from what we have done in the past or even in the present. The first way to ensure this happens is to advertise and communicate the importance of reviewing and compiling lessons learned while conducting initial planning. Everyone involved in planning and execution should know there is a final phase to capture what was done well and what was done poorly. True leaders can recall previous failures and successes when executing. Leaders can do this while everyone else is overly focused on the here and now.

Leaders should apply the same level of intellectual rigor in planning the individual and collective review as they do in planning for the execution of the task. Leaders should review and discuss the entirety of the plan. They should review themselves and their team from actions on *Receive the Task* all the way to *Compile Lessons Learned*. Dominating detail in reviewing the individual and collective should involve all aspects of the plan, not just how you performed the final act. First, the planning phase—what actions did you take when receiving the plan? How was it distributed? Did it provide enough detail? What worked well and what didn't? Why? Next, the preparation phase—once there was a shared understanding of what needed to be completed by what time, how well did we prepare? Did the training match the expectation? Can we say the training resulted in higher performance in execution than if we hadn't done the training? Third, actual execution—did we meet the intent? Why or why not? What didn't we plan for? What do we need to prioritize for next time to ensure a better outcome? Lastly, follow through—as a leader, how are you are holding yourself accountable to the review you just conducted? How are you operationalizing the information you just received? Are you making this information accessible to the greater team so they can benefit from it next time?

There are a couple of different ways to conduct this review. One way is to construct an outline during the planning phase and then refer to it at the end of the event to ensure it keeps you on task with all four phases. Another way is to conduct a review after each phase. Plan and then review how you and your team performed while planning. Train and rehearse, and then review how it went. Execute and then review execution, etc. I would argue that combining the two methods is the best way to compile the most valuable comments and items. Construct a template of how you want this review to be run. It should be a standalone event that requires coordination. Then, conduct a review after each phase or major action throughout the process. You'll find that the amount of detail provided when conducting a review after each phase will be infinitely more valuable than if you only conduct a review at the end of execution. This is because people forget. Leaders should take advantage of the emotional memory associated with recently completing something. The issues, discussions, and recommendations will be much more valuable when you complete these reviews after every phase. Regardless of how you as a leader conduct the review, the worst thing you can do is not conduct a review at all. However, there are some review rules that we should keep in mind.

Leaders should enforce two rules when conducting a review or "hotwash"—professionalism and resiliency. Have the professionalism to understand that no plan is perfect, everyone makes mistakes and could have performed better in something. This is not the time or place to attack individual performance. The review is for the collective before it is for the individual. With that said, we should have the intestinal fortitude to ensure there is no limit to how critical we are of ourselves. If you were responsible for a specific portion of the plan and you hear from multiple people that this portion was not successful or not as good as it could have been, don't take it as a personal attack. If more than one person from separate vantage points brings up the same issue, it's likely valid. Understand that, respect it and learn from it. I imagine these "rules" are why some leaders and organizations do not conduct reviews. They are scared of hurting people's feelings or people focusing on the negative instead of the positive. It's a leader's responsibility to cultivate a professional, resilient, learning organization. If you don't conduct these reviews as a leader, you cannot enforce or expect improvement. It's your responsibility.

MEETINGS: YES — EVERYONE'S FAVORITE

The purpose (why) of a meeting is to synchronize, assess, discuss and distribute. Leaders use meetings as a way to measure individual and collective effectiveness. Meetings are extremely telling. They provide a new leader or a visitor with an immediate glimpse of the organization's culture, discipline, competence, and professionalism. Next time you're in a meeting, pay attention to a few things. Where does the leader sit? What time is the meeting held? How many people speak at the meeting? How many people are present? What's the result? What did the meeting accomplish?

We've all experienced meetings that are more emotional events than they are productive engagements. The size and the speed of an organization is a likely indicator of how many meetings it conducts. I would argue that the larger and faster the organization is, the more meetings they conduct. A leader's calendar is just a compilation of meeting times. As a result of this, meeting performance has become as important as the actual performance. This is a pretty interesting dynamic because some members of the meeting, such as an administrative assistant or a specialty staff member, can only use the meeting to show their performance. Whereas other members of the meeting are present to discuss their own performance or the performance of their team. This means everyone comes to the meeting with a different mindset or expectation. In any case, most people who attend meetings enter the room in some state of nervousness that will affect the entirety of the meeting. One staff member or visitor brings nervousness associated with public speaking or information production. Another staff member brings nervousness associated with the venue or functionality of the room. Does the projector work? Are the slides pulling up? Has the video teleconference (VTC) bridge been established? Is the microphone required? Are there enough chairs? Generally speaking, and depending upon your industry and organization, the only person that isn't nervous is the boss. This is because they are usually the customer of the meeting. They are the most senior person in the room and therefore can take the meeting literally wherever they want. Because of people's fear of being embarrassed in a group setting by their boss or by a peer, they mold their performance around meeting performance, which presents some issues regarding time management, follow through and understanding what's ultimately important. Which is supporting the people you are charged to influence so they can execute the purpose of the organization. Absolutely zero organizations have the purpose of conducting meetings.

Leaders have an inherent responsibility to create an understanding of the value of meetings. If we have realized that meeting performance is part of our actual performance, leaders need to provide expectations for successful, meaningful meetings. The following will provide a breakdown of how to conduct a valuable meeting.

Prior to the meeting: There should be zero confusion as to what the meeting will be about. Organizations that take meetings seriously provide read-ahead documents before the meeting. The purpose of the read-ahead is to ensure a meaningful conversation in the meeting. Everyone involved in the meeting should understand where the meeting will be, what time it will occur and what time it will end. As the leader of the meeting, ask yourself if the meeting needs to occur. If it doesn't, why are you having it? Is there value in meeting anyway just to maintain the cadence or battle rhythm? This is for you to decide.

When: This is completely dependent upon your organization and the type of meeting you would like to conduct, but let's think critically about timing. There is no better time to synchronize the team than at the start of the day. You're able to briefly cover what happened yesterday, the plan for today and beyond. This meeting may also be the only meeting for you as the leader to provide your intent. As discussed, most other meetings are designed *for* the leader, but the morning meeting should be designed *by* the leader. The meeting should be no longer than fifteen minutes, depending on the size of your team. Other aspects to keep in contention for when to schedule meetings, is the time of day. Will the outcomes of the meeting require action by the team? If so, conduct the meeting in the morning hours to give your team enough time to receive the information and adjust. Much like we discussed in the counseling and mentorship session, meetings directly after lunch or at the very end of the day are a terrible idea for the simple reason that people will not be focused on the purpose of the meeting at those times. Don't be that leader. If you're required to attend the meeting, don't be late. Your late arrival will detract from the conversation and flow of the meeting. It also speaks to your professionalism and respect for other leaders.

How: Open the meeting by stating the purpose of the meeting and explaining what will be gained by the end of the meeting. Doing this will keep you and the team on track. Support your statement by providing an agenda. These are things we need to discuss in the time we have allocated for this meeting. There should *always* be a scribe in the meeting. The purpose of this scribe is to compile all notes, leader intent, action items and questions. You may think this is unnecessary because everyone is likely taking notes. True, but they are only compiling notes for things that affect them directly. Your scribe is the catalyst for throughput and clarification! At the end of the meeting, the individual leaders should be repeating back the tasks they were assigned or believe they were assigned. This shows the leader that the task was received and that you are acknowledging accountability for it. After each leader is finished asking clarifying questions, repeating back their individual action items or making final comments, the scribe should vocalize what they captured by section, staff or individual. This will put to bed any confusion and allow the boss or leader to add or subtract from that list before everyone goes their separate ways.

The smaller the meeting, the more personal and involved it will be. Organizations that have daily meetings with more than twenty people at a time are disseminating, not distributing. Which is fine if the intent is to communicate one way. For example, Amazon advertises the "Pizza Rule" in reference to the number of people recommended for a meeting, which I think is awesome. The Pizza Rule is that you never have more people in a meeting than can be fed by two pizzas. There should be no room in your meetings for spectators. Everyone should have a purpose. With that said, leaders would be smart to use meetings as a leadership development tool. What better venue exists to introduce junior leaders or subordinates to the organizations' processes and stakeholders? I would deliberately tell new officers, managers or subordinates to come with me to meetings in the spirit of development. Just allowing them to observe the purpose of a staff, your position and what's important to the boss will significantly improve their perspective—and it costs you absolutely nothing.

The length of the meeting is important as well. Think about how many leaders you may be taking away from their people and overall responsibilities. Any meeting that goes over sixty minutes is a waste of time. People will fill this time with other things whether you know it or not. Ever see the guy who brings one energy drink, one coffee, one water bottle, a full bag of chips and a computer to the meeting? Yeah, that guy is doing something else in your meeting. You'll know that when you ask for his input when it's not his turn to brief and he's got no clue what everyone else in the meeting is discussing. Just be clear about what you expect in your meetings. Of course, there will be times when meetings go over sixty minutes based on the seriousness of the topic and the amount of people in the room, but make this the exception, not the rule.

What: What medium are you using to communicate with one another in the meeting? The go-to for every organization that I have seen is PowerPoint. Others use Excel or some type of tracker filled with a green, amber, red format to show levels of compliance. PowerPoint certainly has its utility and value, but be careful about it becoming a crutch for meetings. The individuals preparing it should be more concerned about the information in it versus the style, font, and aesthetics. What does PowerPoint provide that a whiteboard can't, other than neatness? What about an executive summary or memo? You can fit more content and detail in this medium than in a PowerPoint slide. What topics warrant meetings? This is a leader's decision. Period. Topics should range from leader development, team performance, task compliance and commitment, significant changes, and conditions checks. A leader's discretion and judgment will determine what requires a meeting. As a leader, if you consistently see the same mistakes or tasks being completed to different standards, call a meeting to level the bubbles. If anything above you changes, you owe your team some information. A meeting is a great way to describe change.

Where: Where should meetings be held? Don't rely on a venue to add value to your meeting. Valuable meetings can be held in a vehicle with other team members, on the phone or over lunch. This is directly tied to whatever medium you're using to communicate. Typical meetings are held in some type of board room with comfortable chairs and a projector ready. Usually, everyone is in the room before the boss or leader arrives and they save the seat at the head of the table for the boss. If your leadership style requires that you sit at the head of the table, then you're probably a boss. Leaders can lead from any position around the table.

Meeting Don'ts: Don't be the leader who is consumed with PowerPoint slides. It seems as though PowerPoint construction has become more important than PowerPoint content. Don't get me wrong, I love a great looking PowerPoint slide as much as the next person—I was an Intelligence Officer for God's sake—but I would rather have 1) the correct information 2) and a candid dialog any day of the week. As soon as you start picking apart the font, the few grammatical errors or color of the slides, the person attempting to provide the information is deflated. Make it a learning point of professionalism after the meeting, but don't consume your team's time with spelling and grammar checks. Don't be the person who self-promotes or purposely puts someone else on the spot in the meeting. Some of you can't help yourself. You know the person I am talking about. The person who asks a rhetorical question to a peer loudly enough for everyone to hear and then looks around the room, but specifically towards the boss, for acknowledgment of what they just stated. There is a special place for you on the bottom of the merit list, and you're the only one who doesn't know it. Meetings are not the time or place to list the great things you've done. It's much more appropriate to give thanks to others for supporting you, coax guidance from your leader and highlight the performance of your people.

Post Meeting: This is where meetings become wildly inefficient. Everyone is so relieved to have the meeting completed that they don't follow through on what they said they were going to do. We are also inconsistent with the distribution of information shared or gained from the meeting. Make a habit of distributing what you covered or learned directly after the meeting. The decisions made in the meeting will likely affect everyone in the organization. Distributing these notes directly after the meeting will show your subordinates that you are actively pursuing their concerns, understanding their issues and making the necessary adjustments to make the team better. Use the notes disseminated by the scribe as a tracking mechanism of progress or action. Provide a suspense (due date or time) if an action is required to promote follow-through and completion. Store the data from this meeting in a place where all members can access and use it.

PART IV

LEADER DEVELOPMENT AND TALENT MANAGEMENT

A leader's legacy lies within those they develop. Leaders should measure their success by those they have positively affected and prepared to be future leaders. There is almost nothing more personally and professionally rewarding than observing a junior leader under your charge develop and mature over time. The fulfillment of watching a leader actively employ methods of leadership, patience and emotional intelligence that you have taught them is amazing. When you're able to sit back and watch them lead their people and realize that they are going to be a better leader than you are, you have fulfilled your purpose.

I remember times when people would come to me with an issue or concern while one of my junior leaders was present. Before I could answer or address the persons' concerns, my junior leader would provide a level of guidance and mentorship that left me completely speechless and proud because I could recall when I gave similar guidance to them in the past. I remember looking at them while quietly nodding my head in complete pride and saying to myself, "He's a better leader than I was at that rank or age," or "I'm proud to say that he is better at his job than I am at mine."

Leader development should be a staple of every high-performing organization or individual leader. Both formal and informal methods should be employed to ensure full development. Most times, informal methods are the most influential and genuine because they're usually directly tailored to a person and/or individual topics. Formal methods are critical in providing diverse, all-encompassing topics, and they are the most difficult because they require a deliberate time investment. Organizations and individual leaders who dedicate themselves to this time investment, regardless of their industry, will produce higher quality performance, but more importantly, make better people. Does your organization prioritize the betterment of its people or just the betterment of production? Are they investing time in you or using your time to invest in productivity? Is the development of leaders a priority in your profession or workplace? To be clear, providing job-specific training is not what I'm talking about here. That is process discipline and standard operating procedure for your company or industry. Hopefully, your organization prioritizes leader development at every level. If we're honest with ourselves, most companies do not prioritize leader development in any way. They actively attempt to recruit and retain leaders who have already been developed.

LEADER DEVELOPMENT PROGRAM

A well-constructed leader development program should look like a symmetrical balancing scale with all the leadership senses. It should consist of skill refinement associated with your industry, universal leadership improvement, perspective beyond the normal scope of your industry, and finally, it should be enjoyable to complete and participate in. A leadership development program is different from sporadically conducting leadership development sessions. Leader development sessions, although well-intentioned, are usually given on short notice, have no real measurable improvement metric and usually don't directly contribute to improved leadership performance. I have participated in many leader development sessions, but very few leader developments programs. This should be understandable because the development of a program implies that you, your peers and your superiors are together long enough to justify a program. It implies that your leader prioritizes the development of leaders over everything and that there are enough people within the organization who would benefit from a program versus a session.

The leader development sessions that I have participated in usually involved me being handed a reading list or a title of a book and being told that we were going to discuss what we learned. Sometimes we were told to buy the book, read it all in a week and then come prepared to discuss. Other times, a book was provided to us and we were required to read it over time. The book-only approach to leader development is certainly a step in the right direction, but we should acknowledge that it doesn't provide much breadth or depth. How your leader conducts development should be very telling. It tells you how they prioritize development, how they prioritize their time and it also tells you what they think about your time. I distinctly remember a time when I was told that all the officers were going to conduct a leadership development session while we were deployed that revolved around three or four chapters of a book. I remember being pretty pissed off that my leader thought I had the time available to just casually read something for my development while in a state of execution. I knew I wasn't going to read it based on what I had to prioritize first, but I did appreciate the leader's willingness to prioritize the development of his leaders while in an austere, demanding environment. If a leader who is ultimately responsible for the life and death and the success and failure of thousands of special operations professionals during a time of war can make time to develop their subordinates, we should be thankful. We should also acknowledge that if this leader found the time to develop their leaders, you have absolutely no excuse not to develop yours!

There is no reason why a leader development program cannot be tailored to individual development and organizational betterment. A successful leader development program improves individual and collective performance over time. The time to conduct leader development needs to be deliberately chosen to ensure it's achievable and sustainable. It's one thing to have the intent to conduct leader development. It's another thing to actually do it. Leaders should be inventive when developing a leadership program to ensure the load is shared. Leaders can mitigate canceling program sessions by delegating some of the responsibilities or tasks associated with development sessions. However, don't be the leader who develops a program and just assigns tasks to your subordinates to teach or instruct—it defeats the purpose. It's your program, so own it.

I recommend that leader development programs consist of reading, writing, watching, meeting, leaving and eating.

Reading

Reading is non-negotiable. Leaders are readers. With that said, leadership program developers should be conscious of convenience and quantity. Don't be the leader who makes every subordinate pay fifty dollars for a five-hundred-page book, and think anyone is going to read it for next week or even next month. Stop lying to yourself. Provide the book to those you want to read it. This gives them zero excuses not to have it. Break the book up into sections or chapters. Discuss the sections or chapters and then live the chapters for a week or so. In the next session, have an open dialog about what was experienced.

Writing

Leaders should write well. Effective and purposeful writing provides understanding, analytical detail and sends a message. Leaders who write well send the message that they understand what is asked of them; it provides clear results and highlights performance in a way that is easy to consume and digest. Every high performing organization requires that its leaders write well. Tailor your development program to improve written correspondence. Think about how often leaders are required to convey critical information in the written form. What specific writing requirements does your industry or company contain? Use these as a training tool. Real estate contracts, legal documents, analytical reports, performance evaluations, business proposals, executive summaries, etc. We can all be better writers. Don't be the boss who chooses your best writers to do more than they should because your other subordinates can't do it as well. Train them to success.

Watching

Watching videos, seminars and talks are one of the easiest and most beneficial forms of leader development. Pictures and videos usually provide more context than the written word. It's incredibly easy to find meaningful videos, such as TED talks, when planning a leadership development program. Why paraphrase a speaker or a professional when you can provide the TED talk to your subordinates firsthand? It will introduce them to the sites and locations in which you found the content, which will, in turn, allow the recipient to self-explore and data mine. How do the best professional sports teams in the world prepare to facing other teams and improve? They watch film. Film can be analyzed very closely for individual behavior and collective performance. Take advantage of the information age— it's the easiest investment when developing a program and you'll find that the conversations after are usually very in-depth and genuine.

Meeting

Use your position of influence to build lasting relationships. Introduce your leaders to people, organizations and new experiences. Facilitating connections by inviting others to your meetings and introducing your leaders to people they wouldn't know otherwise will only improve your organization. Someone has the answer to your question—the more people you meet, the more likely you are to get that answer. As much as some people try to make leadership about numbers, leadership will always be about people. Be the leader who brings people together.

Leaving

By leaving, I mean get out of the office! Or wherever it is that you work. Find a frequency that makes sense with your industry and take your leaders out of the workplace to conduct leader development. You will only know a percentage of a person you work with until you can experience them outside of work or their role. If you think about it, the extent of what you know about a person is limited to a building, a floor on that building, or even just a cubical. You shouldn't expect them to know you until they observe you outside of work. Leaders who do this well permanently attach a positive feeling to leadership development, instead of the all-too-familiar, boring, sit in a circle and be talked at method. There are plenty of ways to do this well. If your organization requires some physical performance, it may be appropriate and enjoyable to conduct a physical activity together and find a way that the game you're playing relates to the team's work performance. Another example of this would be thinking of a way to promote physical activity while finding a healthy way to relieve stress or release tension, even if a professional work topic is never discussed. By doing this, you are still developing the team for the greater good.

Once, as a staff officer, while deployed, I noticed that the staff and the command team were constantly at each other's throats. This particular deployment involved a new leader, which resulted in a learning curve for the staff that was palpable and painful. That type of environment is already one of extreme stress and risk. The fact that each leader within the organization was becoming increasingly bitter required some alleviation of stress, and I assessed the alleviation needed to be immediate. I schemed with the other staff officers and got them to agree to bring our new leader to a meeting to explain an operational capability that he hadn't been briefed on yet. However, in reality, I planned for a tent the size of an airplane hangar to be secured and saved for us to use. I deliberately chose a time for us to conduct this "brief" to mitigate him catching wind of my plan. After about twenty straight hours of work, I gathered the other staff officers I conspired with and grabbed our new leader. Once I got them all in the tent, I dropped two bags of rubber kicks balls on the floor and said we're going to play dodgeball. Everyone turned into children for thirty minutes. We were able to take out all of our frustrations by attempting to kill each other with rubber balls that were heavy enough to break your nose if they connected right. We all left wearing smiles and we walked back into our workspace motivated to work for each other towards a common goal. It is still pretty funny to think about how violent and competitive a dodge ball game can get between Rangers. Other examples of "leaving" that I have seen work well have been visiting battlefields, museums, think-tanks, and other Fortune 500 companies for leadership and business best practices.

Eating

Never underestimate the value of breaking bread with people. Breaking bread with people is an age-old tradition that facilitates comradery and peace. You may not agree on a business method or practice, but we can all agree on good food and the conversations that ensue will present commonalities and bring us closer together. Conversations that happen over food are revealing and sometimes personal. They give us a glimpse of who people are versus what we see at work or in a strictly professional setting. I would make it point once a week to share a meal with my junior leaders to gauge how they were doing personally and how the organization was running from their perspective. These conversations were invaluable to me because they would start with the meal itself, evolve into our personal lives and naturally flow to work. Don't be the leader that's business every time, all the time. It sends the message that you don't care about who your junior leaders are. Our once-a-week meal was usually breakfast after a physical event, where we also gained an appreciation for each other. Working hard physically and following it with a meal meant that in a few hours we were able to learn a lot about each other and transition into more serious work-related topics that affected both the individual and the collective. During these breakfasts, I would learn about myself, how I was perceived, what we were doing well and what I needed to make the organization understand better. I would reciprocate by providing performance feedback to my subordinate leaders, explaining the implications of work decisions or candidly explaining challenges I was facing to give them an idea of leadership issues at my level. I can say with confidence that my most valuable conversations with junior leaders usually happened over a meal.

You can learn a lot about a person by what and how they eat. The calorie counting, food separating, precision knife cutting person probably shows attributes like this at work. For this person, every condition has to be planned as perfectly as possible; these people may be frugal and disciplined. Whereas those who are more liberal with what they eat, and the ones who chew, speak and laugh with a full mouth of food, may be willing to assume risk while making decisions. They may roll with the punches and live by the motto that life is short, so make it fun. With that said, don't over-analyze this. Breaking bread with people should be a way to build a bridge between people and organizations. How many times have you heard about a business meeting or an engagement make zero headway until the meal and drinks afterward? The intent is not to get people liquored up, but a way to establish a personal, long-lasting relationship. This is why I imagine any salesperson, from any industry, is quick to bring potential clients to dinner. Make it about the relationship. If you can teach and learn while having a meal, everyone involved will be pleased and made better for it.

If you insert reading, writing, watching, meeting, leaving and eating into a leadership development program, you'll know your people, which means you'll know how to influence them. Apply these six leader development techniques to your calendar to establish a sustainable leader development program. Once you establish the frequency in holding these events, compile content for each technique. Content for your leadership development program should almost bombard you. When compiling content for your leadership development program, you should keep two things in contention at all times. First, being a leader is the most important position that anyone will ever hold. Two, never do anything for just one purpose. With these in mind, you'll start to notice opportunities to help develop those around you everywhere. You'll notice them while completing other meaningful work. For example, when assigned to a project, you'll likely be introduced to new processes and people in the completion of that task. Maintain those contacts, keep a log of what you've learned and add these people and lessons to your leadership development program. You'll begin to realize that your mind will start to naturally envision ways to develop others. A book, a video, a venue, etc. can be applied to your leadership development program. When you begin to do this over time, you'll notice the content you've compiled for your leadership development program will become more valuable and diverse, and therefore more sustainable.

There are many different ways you can employ these six leader development techniques over time, but you must be flexible in their frequency and implementation. The easiest way to employ them would be to cover one technique per week. If you were to compile nine samples or topics for each technique, you would be able to sustain a leader development program for fifty-four weeks. Keep in mind that not every technique requires a completely new start or topic. A meeting that you conduct can span more than two sessions or a video that you're watching can be split apart over multiple weeks. This will save you time and effort as you continue to complete the necessary and required tasks associated with your job or profession. You can also assign and delegate some of these techniques to your subordinate leaders over time to develop *their* ability to coordinate with others, practice their planning skills, hone their presentation skills, etc. Your leadership intent should not only be to provide the recipients with leadership content but also to teach them how to develop their own leadership development program. Before you realize it, you'll be impressed with what they compile, and leader development will become a known and recurring battle rhythm event that adds significant value to your team for years after you've left the position.

Another way to insert a leader development program into your organization is to combine it with your review of work performance (again, never do anything with just one purpose). If you're the type of organization that reviews its performance, which every organization should be, you can use the time associated with review to improve individual and collective leadership techniques. For example, while in an operations role within a Fortune 500 company, I would sacrifice at least one to two hours a week in the name of team improvement, review, and development. I would gather the team in a conference room and we would openly discuss our performance on a whiteboard. I would lead the team through discussing what we learned from that week's performance, and what our goals were for the next week, distribute plans I received for future projects, compile recommendations or concerns made by my subordinates leaders, cover one chapter of a leadership book and then finish the session on a high note by playing some type of game to build the team's cohesion and morale. As result, our work performance improved significantly, and our leaders became the type of leaders that made recommendations for the problems they encountered. They were candid in their feedback and developed a sense of team that increased communication, trust, and overall performance.

The byproduct of a sustainable leader development program is talent management. The greater the amount of valuable time spent with leaders in the execution of a leadership development program, the better your ability will be to assess talent. Talent management is the ability to identify talent, recruit talent and retain talent. You'll be able to identify talent beyond work performance by observing leadership potential. For example, while executing a leader development session, you may hear about a decision or action made by a subordinate or employee. You'll start to notice that you'll hear this person's name more than once. Once this happens, you may have just identified talent. This cues you, as a leader, to observe this person more closely. In your observation, you confirm what your direct subordinates have said about this person and look for ways to internally promote or empower this person with more responsibility. You counsel this person and provide them feedback regarding their consistently high performance and encourage them to seek positions of more responsibility and leadership. You just recruited talent. Over time, you notice their individual competence, performance, and potential is valuable to the team. It's your responsibility to continuously challenge and support this person. You make a deliberate leadership investment into this person for the good of the person and the company while actively looking for ways to support their continued progression. When this person realizes that your interest in their development goes beyond company productivity, or learn that you have their best interest in mind, you just retained that talent.

SUMMARY

Leaders are not born, they are developed. Although I believe the best leaders are groomed from an early age and are exposed to all aspects of life, it's never too late to develop your leadership potential or the leadership potential of others. All people need leadership and even leaders need to be led. Some say that people are owed great leaders. I would argue that it is just as important to have weak leaders because of what's learned as a result. Leaders must know how and when to be led before they know how and when to lead. Our first leaders are usually our parents or parental figures. Our next leaders are usually coaches and teachers, but all leaders regardless of position or industry are also coaches and teachers. Learn as much as you can from whoever has something to offer—and everyone has something to offer, whether it be the right or wrong example. Our best leaders are often our most observant people. While observing and learning, they can see themselves objectively, know how they are perceived and are relatable because they have exposed themselves to all types of people in society.

I believe we can make a more deliberate effort to groom future leaders in our young people. Our most experienced leaders should bear this responsibility by sharing their experiences and wisdom. In many cultures, this is already happening. This is the reason why most cultures cherish their elderly or elders. They have simply lived long enough to experience so many facts of life that they can tell history's perspective. We know that history repeats itself, whether it involves the cause of war, the pendulum of political views or the cyclical nature of seasons. We would be smart to study our history's leaders, regardless of country or religion, because we'll experience their challenges again and again. We should educate our future leaders to be culturally aware, educationally diverse, hard-working and ready. We should train them for the world we live in and the world we're leaving them.

No doubt our school systems attempt to do this, but they are slow to provide updated information and knowledge. They focus on fundamental, historic information as opposed to practical life lessons and only really prepare our youth for further education available to the highest bidders with an end state of acquiring the highest-paying job possible. I do not doubt that our education administrators have our children's best interests in mind, but we should agree that we need to supplement the baseline education they receive to prepare them for the realities of life and leadership. I propose that a leadership academy designed to prepare our youth for the harsh realities of life will significantly improve leader development for the future. Our youth should be exposed to and trained in overall wellness—physical wellness, environmental wellness, mental wellness, and life wellness.

The intent of physical wellness is to establish individual discipline. Introducing our youth to physical fitness will prepare them for things more difficult, such as mental toughness, resiliency, and adversity. With our ever-increasing knowledge of the human body, we should educate our youth and future leaders to care for themselves first so they can care for others later, as leaders. The sense of individual accountability and role establishment will later lend itself to team building and unity. Preparing these leaders to experience physical struggle in controlled environments will prepare them for much more difficult life situations.

Environmental wellness teaches our future leaders the importance of conservation, agricultural importance, and nutrition. Our society is backward regarding environmental awareness. We spend our make-pretend currency on inanimate objects, such as vehicles and clothes, instead of quality food. We have forgotten about the skill, work ethic and delicacy of agriculture. Most of us eat purely out of enjoyment, convenience or taste versus nutrition or sustenance. We should teach our children the effects of what we eat, where it comes from and what food provides—beyond what it tastes like. We should instill a diet that is as deliberate and disciplined as our work lives and school lives. We should teach our future leaders how to sustain themselves, how to grow crops that we have since taken advantage of and their importance to the earth. These lessons will make our future leaders physically healthier, environmentally conscious, less wasteful and considerate of our resources.

Mental wellness is where we all stand to grow and improve the most. The foundation laid from physical and environmental wellness will prepare our future leaders to be more mindful and self-aware. Teaching our future leaders to think critically about their thinking will facilitate improved concentration, focus, and consciousness. Recent studies and more progressive schools have already reported increases in performance and behavior in young students who meditate at least once a day. Think about the headway we could make if we were to embrace this type of mental wellness in all students. I believe we would produce leaders who are more spiritually aware, educated and accepting of others.

Life wellness is about preparing our future leaders for reality. We all who people that prepare their children to chase dreams that less than

1% of the world's population will ever acquire, such as becoming a professional athlete. It is perfectly acceptable and healthy to encourage our youth to attack their dreams, but that does not absolve us of preparing the future for the knowns of life. You will pay taxes, you will have to be smart with money, you will have to work for a living, and most of us will have to do things we have absolutely no passion for to make that living. These are facts. Let's embrace these facts and prepare future leaders to dominate these details. First, let's teach them how to work with their hands. Why wouldn't we do this? To some, it's because they think they are above it. They believe only the uneducated or delinquent work with their hands. If you believe this, your thought process is inherently flawed. How can you begin to think you add value or creation to the world in a position that ultimately means absolutely nothing in the grand scheme? If the world were to end today, how would you explain the purpose and value of your position? We would be smart to teach our youth to create things with their hands from the resources the earth provides us. Learning to be a mason, a carpenter or farmer is internationally important and ageless. At the absolute minimum, wouldn't it teach our youth what they may have to do if they didn't finish their "higher" education? The humility, interpersonal skills and work ethic that our future leaders will acquire while learning a trade will last them a lifetime. It will teach them patience, the art of creation and the ease of destruction.

I can say with confidence that I never formally learned how to save, spend or invest money. No one ever helped me understand the stock market or what does debt is. Much like anything else, we usually learn the fastest when we make a mistake and it causes pain. We need to prepare our future leaders for the complexity of our monetary systems and processes. Unfortunately, money is the reason, end state, and purpose for most actions. I wish it wasn't true, but it is. The more we teach our future leaders to manage their money well, the less likely they are to be scared of it. The industries and institutions we pay don't want us to know as much as they do, because it'll cost them their gluttonous livelihood. We see examples of how the insanely wealthy become that way off of the backs of others. The only way to combat or eliminate this fact of life is to arm our future leaders with education, hands-on experience and guidance.

The words servanthood and volunteerism mean very little to most people today. When is the last time you volunteered your time or yourself to anything? This is not rolling your window down half an inch at a stoplight to drop a quarter in a bucket for the homeless. This means true dedication to serving something bigger than yourself. How can you teach your children and aspiring leaders to do this without ever doing it yourself? In this regard, most people live by the creed "do as I say, not as I do." If it were up to me, all Americans would have to serve in some capacity for two years. Whenever I say this to people, they almost melt—it is truly hilarious to me. On a serious note, it's also concerning. To think that you are better than serving something greater than yourself is the true mark of you having no idea how the world works or how incredibly lucky you are to be living in it.

By service, I mean serving in some type of organization with a mission to contribute to the national or global wellbeing. The most recognizable form of service would be military service, but I also mean in other capacities, such as forest services, environmental protection services, the US Postal Service, waste management, and as a teacher, police officer or firefighter. These agencies and professions are critical to our country functioning but are incredibility undervalued and underpaid, which is why it's difficult to identify, recruit and retain talent into them. Put simply, servanthood and volunteerism should be hard. The reward for that hard work is appreciation and contribution. We should encourage our children and young leaders to volunteer their time and effort to valiant efforts at nursing homes, hospitals, local clubs, etc. The perspective gained will last beyond a lifetime. Service of something greater will simply put you in your rightful place in the world and let you know exactly where you stand. If you think this is too grandiose, an easier, more practical display of servanthood, volunteerism and humility is cleaning. Yes, no one is above it. Most young and aspiring leaders don't appreciate what it takes to maintain something or an area. Once they are done using something or some place for the desired purpose, hand them a mop and bucket. Teach them to leave it better than they left it. It serves a purpose greater than themselves and teaches them discipline, humility, and perspective.

LEADERSHIP WAY AHEAD

In an ideal world, our bosses and chief executives are the leaders we discuss in this book. Unfortunately, though, we know this is very rarely the case. As a result, organizations and their people experience a consistent ebb and flow of quality leaders, managers and bosses, all of who prioritize something different, if anything at all. The nature of some of our industries sometimes calls for technicians to be placed in leadership positions and we watch as organizational performance plummets due to micromanagement or a lack of true leadership. Fortune 500 companies have attempted to mitigate this by hiring vetted and tested leaders, but there are usually more positions available than there are real leaders to fill them. Or the leader is never in position long enough to truly affect change, improvement or leader development. Fortune 500 companies would be wise to acknowledge the commodity of leadership and establish a deliberate branch or section dedicated to leadership at all levels of the business.

Imagine if a Chief Leadership Officer (CLO) were an added member to the senior team of your company. The purpose of that CLO would be to establish leadership development programs and best practices to professionalize your force and contribute to productivity. Adjacent to and subordinate of the CLO would be a dedicated team attached to every echelon or level of your company. Those leadership professionals would advise your operators and staff at their respective levels. To ensure the CLO position isn't hamstrung by the operations or staff contingent, they would report directly to an echelon above the level they are working. This will prevent on-site leaders or operations officers from minimizing leadership efforts and authority. However, that CLO and the leadership staff need to understand that just because they do not answer directly to someone in the operations section or staff doesn't mean they are absolved of team support and collaboration. Their sole purpose is to support the operational process and the person designated to manage the entirety of the site or operational task.

Establishing a leadership specific section within a company would likely provide multiple benefits. These leadership professionals would be responsible for providing truly candid feedback to company seniors and managers based upon feedback received from the company's workforce. Their operational contribution would be to professionalize the operational leaders by developing comprehensive leader development programs to improve leadership attributes, planning, and professionalism. They would standardize leadership training initiatives, preparing operational leaders for their responsibilities and creating a shared understanding of leadership progression. They could represent your location or branch by visiting other company locations and garnering feedback, operational best practices and leadership best practices. They would educate your operators and staff on communication and counseling techniques. They would provide inventive ways of team building, morale building, and cohesion. They would compile the lessons learned from previous performance and courses of action for correction to improve future performance. They would be the buffer between the human dimension and delivering results. This agency of leaders would be like having your own leadership consultants who are emotionally unattached to the company's operational performance but are wed to the company's leadership professionalization.

FINAL THOUGHTS / CLOSING

True leaders need to know almost nothing about the business to effect positive change. The process of your business isn't nearly as important as you think it is. True leaders significantly contribute to your organization quickly by immediately investing in people, bringing a beginner's mind to any problem and garnering feedback to create ownership. Your company likely pays a lot of people who are, or have become, subject matter experts, but subject matter experts rarely inspire others to achieve something great. Leaders work *for* the people, and as a result become a known and trusted commodity, sometimes before managers who have been with the company for a decade. They earn loyalty and trust by learning from everyone, regardless of position, and actively pursue the recommendations of others to make the organization better. They can swallow their pride, change their mind often and fail without embarrassment. They remember people's names, their ideas and act upon them. They spend time doing the task that every member of the company must do. They are hard to find in office spaces because they would rather be experiencing what the companies' employees experience and they look at the calendar, not at the clock.

Being a leader is the most important role that a person will ever fill. It shouldn't be confused with being a boss or a manager. Leaders are common people that influence other people to achieve uncommon goals. Leaders don't need to be the fastest, strongest, oldest, smartest or richest people. They must simply be self-aware, observant, humble, interpersonal and hard-working. All leaders have weaknesses, and no two leaders are ever the same. We should be hard-pressed to find "a favorite leader" because so many people in history and the present provide incredible examples of leadership. The best leaders do not need to be leaders of countries, armies or the world's richest companies. The best leaders are quick to minimize their contributions and often point to the men and women around them for their leadership reputation. My last recommendation for how to approach leadership is to remind yourself every day that somewhere a mother or a father has unknowingly trusted you, and no one else, to nurture, protect and lead their children. There is no greater honor or responsibility (nor will there ever be) than providing leadership to our future.

CPSIA information can be obtained
at www.ICGtesting.com
Printed in the USA
BVHW042342170820
586599BV00007B/213